LIVE EXPERIENCES TO
ACCELERATE YOUR JOURNEY

FAST >> FORWARD TO FACILITATION

A COLLECTIVE BY
NINE AUTHORS

PRACTICAL INSIGHTS FOR FACILITATORS, BUSINESS LEADERS AND HR PROFESSIONALS

Turquoise Publication

INDIA • SINGAPORE • MALAYSIA

Notion Press Media Pvt Ltd

No. 50, Chettiyar Agaram Main Road,
Vanagaram, Chennai, Tamil Nadu – 600 095

First Published by Notion Press 2021
Copyright © Arvind Murwaha, Nasreen Khan, Nitin Welde,
Parineeta Mehra, Shubha Rajan, Sushma Banitha, Varsha Chitnis,
Vasudha Lal, Yateen Gharat 2021
All Rights Reserved.

ISBN 978-1-63904-731-4

This book has been published with all efforts taken to make the material error-free after the consent of the authors. However, the authors and the publisher do not assume and hereby disclaim any liability to any party for any loss, damage, or disruption caused by errors or omissions, whether such errors or omissions result from negligence, accident, or any other cause.

While every effort has been made to avoid any mistake or omission, this publication is being sold on the condition and understanding that neither the authors nor the publishers or printers would be liable in any manner to any person by reason of any mistake or omission in this publication or for any action taken or omitted to be taken or advice rendered or accepted on the basis of this work. For any defect in printing or binding the publishers will be liable only to replace the defective copy by another copy of this work then available.

Praise for Fast Forward to Facilitation

'The stories in this book demonstrate that, I know several of the contributors and have learned with them in some of the courses I have done in India or now virtually. All of the stories are powerful, and I really appreciate their willingness to share their journey in all aspects. Keep your eyes open for the "cracked" pot and the "big bindi" two of many stories that I really liked and that speak to what we can each learn by paying attention to our own journey.

This book has bits that will speak to facilitators at different places in their development. It is written by facilitators who while all are competent each has gotten there in very different ways. Like all facilitators they are still on the journey, but they are taking a minute to share. Stories are about "my" journey shared in a way that speaks to each of us. The diversity seems to guarantee that several will speak to you wherever you are in your path of facilitation. —*Larry Philbrook CPF CTF, ICA Taiwan*

'Facilitation anthology does what it is meant to do – act as a catalyst and point of reference for many aspiring facilitators. Logical categorization of discussion points captures the readers' interest to delve more into the art of facilitation. The informal writing style makes reading a pleasant experience and the authors have carefully blended both time-tested concepts and contemporary thoughts to drive home their point. Narration is erudite and succinct, and the anecdotes make the reading all the more captivating. This book is an effective tool for academicians of higher education institutions and others who care to make a difference to them and make an indelible impact on others' lives.' —*Dr. Uma Warrier, Professor (OB & HR) and Area Coordinator CMS B School, Jain University*

'This is an interesting book, not just for wanting to be facilitators, but for practitioners at large! Facilitation skills are used by leaders even today (perhaps unknowingly) to manage large teams and businesses. And these will become increasingly important in improving the effectiveness of cross functional teams in non-hierarchical structures.' —*Neeraj Swaroop, Ex Regional CEO (India and South East Asia), Standard Chartered Bank.*

'The compiled book by nine experienced facilitators pins and bowls over excellent Facilitation techniques by taking the reader's hand and walking step-by-step through their journey of real-life examples. The masterful book shares knowledge, understanding and methodologies on all aspects of facilitation that can enrich facilitators to lead and support complex business transformation initiatives, change management, start-up programs and any effective interventions.' —*Mohan Kumar, Global Practise Head, WIPRO Ltd*

'*Fast Forward to Facilitation* is indeed a unique collection of thought provoking stories. While the book is aimed towards facilitators, the dominant thought it left on me is that it's ideally suited to CXOs & Leaders who want to progress in today's time of unprecedented uncertainties. Having led large multinational organizations for decades and now mentoring & putting up bootstrap start-ups, I realize that the ideas in the book have big potential in terms of equipping leaders to excel. I believe that an effective leader has got to be a highly skilled facilitator. That's what will create crucial value add to the teams & companies. The book has helped me to reflect & pick up some ideas best suited to my facilitation style & hope it helps you as well. Congratulations & kudos to the nine authors for putting together the string of ideas so very well!' —*Rakesh Sarin, Founder of Nyshaasa Energy; Former: CEO. Suzlon Energy & Global President, Energy Solutions of Wartsila Corp, Finland.*

'Fast Forward to Facilitation is a unique compilation of nine inspiring stories, each depicting the facilitation journey of accomplished professionals from different walks of life. These stories, though independent, weave together to constitute a powerhouse of techniques of facilitation, in an interesting and engaging format. In each of the stories, authors talk about their struggles, their own realizations and learnings from the situations they faced and have nicely outlined their journey towards their professional and personal growth. It demonstrates the fact that facilitation techniques could be used across sectors, equally effectively. If you are already in the field of facilitation, this provides you with some powerful tips to fast forward the impact of your facilitation.' —*Dr. Rajeev Ranjan, An HR Professional in a CEO role, Head-South Asia, Rotary International.*

Contents

Foreword 9

Introduction 11

Learning and Unlearning Facilitation
    Varsha Chitnis 17

Facilitation to the Rescue!
    Varsha Chitnis 28

'Facilitatee 2 Facilitator'
    Shubha Rajan 35

I am POSH!
    Shubha Rajan 48

The Experiential Facilitator
    Arvind Murwaha 53

Facilitating Results
    Arvind Murwaha 66

Whose Game is it Anyway!
    Vasudha Lal 73

In the Light of a Day
    Vasudha Lal 84

The Learning Curve to Facilitation
    Parineeta Mehra..91

Riding the Wave to New Shores
    Parineeta Mehra..104

Facilitative Air Warrior
    Nitin Welde..111

Facilitation Has Impact
    Nitin Welde..124

Nirvana through Facilitation
    Sushma Banthia..131

Desired Outcome
    Sushma Banthia..143

The Facilitation Expedition
    Yateen Gharat..151

The Covid Saga
    Yateen Gharat..164

Nuts, Bolts, and Jolts
    Nasreen Khan..171

The Infinite End
    Nasreen Khan..182

Power Tips to Help You Fast Forward *187*
Glossary *197*
Acknowledgements..*201*

Foreword

Sanjay Dugar
(India Chair, IAF)

Facilitation has the power to create a huge positive impact, sometimes even surpassing what the stakeholders may have imagined. This I am saying out of what I was fortunate enough to experience.

I was enamored with facilitation when I first came across a 5-member Japanese delegation that presented their story of how they helped Japan recover from a Tsunami and a nuclear disaster that occurred simultaneously. While Japan may have had great recovery stories of the past, this one was special because it showcased how structured conversations and interactions between groups of people could rebuild hope amongst people, build courage to fight back, align to work together in an effective way, and get more out of less – more positive impact with fewer resources. This inspired me to tread the journey of learning to facilitate, and it changed my life.

I soon realized that there was a lot more than just learning the skills and tools of facilitation, and it actually is a journey – an enjoyable one at that – towards *being* a facilitator. While this skill has helped me create an impact for my stakeholders, it also gave me a new way of living my life. It brought into me a sense of joy – happiness is momentary, but joy is permanent. It taught me how to really harness the power of collective group wisdom and show that the power of a group is far greater than combined individual strengths.

This book brings out the journey of nine impact-creating facilitators, who so nobly have shared their stories of how they embarked on their journey of becoming a facilitator and have also shared some joyous moments of the impact they have created. The diversity of the authors is an added advantage for the readers, as it showcases a variety of ways to use facilitation skills, and even how to build on it. I sincerely wish that their tribe grows multi-fold, the world needs them.

This book also showcases impact stories that could provide some deep insights to corporate leaders and HR folks on how they could make use of it to drive change and further their businesses. For readers thinking about how they could become facilitators and play their role in creating a positive impact, stories of these nine accomplished facilitators about their journey may show you some way forward. For those who are practicing facilitators, and the ones that are new to it, the stories showcasing impact that they have created could inspire us to do more.

Let us all go out there and create the impact that is needed, and even more so in this post-pandemic era, where we need to provide relief, rehabilitate, rebuild the world, and take it to a new level of glory.

– **Sanjay Dugar**
India Chair, 2020–2022
International Association of Facilitators (IAF)

Introduction

"Experience is the teacher of all things."

– Julius Caesar

Being an effective facilitator is a lifelong journey. A journey that seems simple and easy, but requires clear direction and guidance. A journey that, for most facilitators, takes a long time to traverse – decades and sometimes a lifetime!

Why do facilitators struggle in their journey? What can help facilitators – new or seasoned – to speed up this journey? There is so much literature available today on facilitation. A lot of research has also happened. And yet, facilitators struggle to get it right. There seems to be some lacuna, some gap that hasn't been plugged yet. What exactly is that? This became the genesis of our book.

As facilitators from diverse backgrounds, we realized there were some common roadblocks we all faced. Despite our very varied journeys, there seemed to be a common thread of mistakes and realizations. One echo common to us all was: "I wish I had known this earlier".

We set about creating a resource that helps overcome this challenge. There is a lot written about facilitative techniques and processes. What has been missing is the real-life application of these techniques and processes. We realised that each of us had learnt through our individual experiences. And most of the times, experience teaches lessons the hard way. We have come together to pen our experiences and journeys thus far, simply because of the impact we have witnessed as we worked more and more through facilitation. These experiences are game changers and change makers.

When we started sharing our experiences with each other, we were fascinated to discover the wide array of events where facilitation had worked seamlessly. As per the Cambridge dictionary, facilitation means, "the process of making something possible or easier". In the corporate world, facilitation is frequently associated with learning. Our stories talk about that, and then take you further. They will tell you how it has been applied across sectors and situations. How facilitation can make decision-making smoother. How it can ease problem solving – possibly bringing a wider range of solutions. How facilitation can lead to a more engaged group with more ideas and viewpoints getting expressed. In fact, each of us has used facilitation for different purposes.

Applications of facilitation go beyond the corporate world as well. In one story, you will discover how it helped a community to overcome their challenges. In another, you may find it used in a school setting. In yet another, you may discover it being used in all areas of life!

The question to ponder over is, how does it work in these varied situations? What goes wrong when it does not work? How will it work for you in a practical sense? What are the things to look out for?

In sharing our journey, we open doors to what has worked practically for us. And what did not work for us. You can steer away from the pitfalls we had. Our wish is that as a facilitator, you can create the wins for yourself faster and easier.

We believe, this book is the first of its kind. The nine of us are from diverse backgrounds: IT professional, Mountain climber, Air Force veteran, Sales Leader, L&D professional, Educator, HR Leader and Coach. We bring together more than 250 years of collective experience, all so different and yet we all have created our success as facilitators. This book shares our journeys and what it takes to go through the grind. It shares how we used facilitation in real life. How each one of us found our North Star is a unique tale in this space.

So, through our experiences you will get to know where all facilitation has and can work (and we are still discovering more too!). You will learn about the impact facilitation creates. Impact on people, Impact on institutions, Impact on business. You will be able to pick up the nuances of facilitation. The principles of facilitation remain the same. What is different is the manner in which these principles manifested for each one of us. Each one of us has used the art and science of facilitation in our own unique way.

Whether you are new to facilitation, or you have dabbled with it, this book will help you shape your journey as a facilitator and give it a better direction. It will accelerate your 'learning curve'. The manner in which it has been written it will be easy for you to read, comprehend and follow. Each facilitator has shared the journey their lives have taken before, during, and after discovering facilitation. We have also shared a particular incident that has stood out and made a huge impact not only on our lives as facilitators, but also on people who experienced the power of facilitation. We hope you gain as much insight while reading as we did while writing these for you.

As a diverse group of facilitators, we had our own journey of writing this book. In penning this book we could not meet up in person. All our discussions and brainstorming had to be on virtual platforms – on video conferences and messaging platforms only. We shared interests. We jotted down notes. Each one of us volunteered to take up some responsibility. We had to agree and disagree though these virtual means of communication. This is when we felt most grateful to have learnt to use facilitated conversations. We connected with each other as buddies. Everyone helped everyone. This "dance of facilitation" has been very enriching for us all in many ways.

As facilitators, we are all still learning and growing. Join us on this journey!

Happy Reading!

Varsha Chitnis

An entrepreneur, change coach, facilitator, facilitative trainer, visiting faculty with B-schools, she works with management, the c-suite, and teams to build cultures of growth, learning, accountability and collaboration. Enabling mindset changes for transition and transformation is her forte. Facilitating conversations on crisis management, vision creation and alignment, functional coordination and working with diverse cross culture virtual teams to be inclusive is what she has been doing.

Learning and Unlearning Facilitation

Varsha Chitnis

"Hey! I object to the title of your session. You seem to be stereotyping people." This remark hit me like a bolt from the blue. It had just not occurred to me. The group fell silent. I felt numb. The group spoke about it a little longer and moved ahead to the next step. I heard a voice say that there is no space left on this wall for our ideas. What do we do now? I turned to look at the wall full of coloured papers with ideas. As I looked up, everything came to a halt. I felt a sudden rush of heat in my face, my ears and nose felt hot, my heart was going thud, thud! I just stood there blank. I had not anticipated this logistical challenge. One participant came forward with masking tape. He started taping long strips on one side of the wall. Another participant followed his lead. Soon, each idea remaining was up on the wall! I felt spared. Trying hard to keep a calm face, I continued. I asked questions to move the group towards the outcome. It seemed like nothing had gone wrong.

I experienced this incident at the 6th Annual International Association of Facilitators Conference at Delhi in 2019. As a first-time conference facilitator, I felt excited yet nervous. The experience left a deep mark on me. I realised what it is to be vulnerable. I realised it is not easy to be present and tuned in to what is happening now. I am aware I had struggled to be present as a facilitator that day. How could I have dealt with the situation differently? How could I have facilitated what was emerging at the moment, better? Each time I think of these questions, different answers come up. I am still learning.

As a 10-year-old, I felt important that I was a part of a big family decision: the decision to choose a name for my baby brother. Eager to go first, I said, "I choose Kartik and Rohan because they are short, and I like them." My sister followed with her choice, 'Jatin.' Dad shared his list and said, "I like Rohan and Jatin". "I can't decide yet," was mom's response. We decided to vote. We were all happy. How we arrived at this decision is etched in my memory. I did not know then that we had used a facilitation process. The fact that we participated in this decision as equals mattered the most. Choosing to be silent is a contribution, I learned. An individual's choice needs to be respected. What mattered the most was that I felt included. My contribution was valued. I know that this is fundamental to any meaningful conversation. I am mindful of this and *value each contribution* when I facilitate.

When in middle school, I was a member of the social studies club. Our club had only 6 of us as members. We took up a challenge to participate in the first-ever exhibition organized by our school. We took turns to lead brainstorms, plan and draw a budget for the material. One day, we were feeling low. Walking into the playground, my friend started writing her ideas one by one on the mud with stones. We followed her. After a good 20-odd minutes, we were able to connect our ideas. We circled similar ones. Crossed the ones that were opposite ideas and ticked those that went together. It felt good. Some of our energy started coming back. Then on another patch of mud, we put similar ideas together and drew a border to box them. We named each box and created categories. Once the groups were clear, we were able to make decisions on what we needed to start. We got help from other clubs and built our models and exhibits and put up a good show.

Now, 35 years later, I know we had used facilitation. We had used sorting, clustering, chunking, and categorizing. At that time, it made a lot of sense to our teenage minds. The beauty of this process was that each one of us was involved. We took it upon ourselves to make our exhibition a success. Our bond was strong. We also learned to respect other views. The focus was on creating something new. It was the power of facilitation. I can now say.

While leading projects in college, I wondered how I could get my friends and seniors to agree. How would I get everyone to follow the group's norms? Haven't we all experienced this as a leader? In my experience, conversations enhance team bonding. The sense of being connected comes with listening, asking questions, and sharing. As the rapport increases, conversations deepen and become more inclusive. Differences are valued. It is about creating a safe space for everyone to be themselves. Living in different parts of India made me tolerant and sensitive to diversity. Are these not some essential behaviours of a facilitator? For me, *Inclusion creates a space for everyone to express.*

*

After my graduation in Commerce and Law, we moved to Mumbai and I found myself challenged by the pace and competitiveness of Mumbai. I enrolled in a professional program to become a Company Secretary. I thought then that I wanted to be a part of the corporate boardroom and contribute to the business. I wanted to experiment with other things too. One day, an opportunity to work and understand the dealing of the stock exchange came in. I jumped in, not knowing about stocks and trading. Soon, I started managing the all-India sub-brokers network of the main broker at the Bombay Stock Exchange. My role required me to interact with sub-brokers from across the country. I started practicing bits of facilitation now.

I learned to set expectations, ensure compliance, and design an effective communication system. It increased the speed and accuracy of daily trade transactions. Influencing the stakeholders through telephonic conversations and fax messages was challenging. It taught me to connect and understand others. It is so critical to manage expectations and performances in business. I acquired the ability to hold space for others, to express, and to be accepting of what the group decided. As the only woman managing this network, my facilitation approach helped me. It was at this moment that I realized how much it meant to me to have human interactions and enable conversations. The stocks and trade did not excite me as much as the telephonic conversations with people. I realized that this was what I wanted to continue doing. Soon, I got introduced to experiential learning and found my passion!

*

Back in Mumbai, a year later, I started my career as a behavioural trainer. That day I dressed in a saree, sporting a 'big bindi' to look the part of an experienced trainer. I was at the Mahanagar Telephone Exchange at Dockyard road. My participants were senior officers who were due to retire. They were more than two times my age and more experienced. I was nervous. I checked the transparency projector (those were the transparency days) several times. As I warmed up to get into module 1, the electric supply to that floor stopped. My worst fears were a reality. With no electricity and no transparencies! What could I do? The only thing that I could think of was to have a conversation with the participants. "Would you all be willing to form groups on your own?" I asked. There was more energy now in the room. The activity and debrief went off well. Each person in the room participated. They were all playing around like children.

It helped me build rapport with the group and the next two days flew by. I realised that adults need to speak, share, listen and act to learn. Again, I had used rapport to gain support from this group. The second learning for me was that of always having a plan B in place. I decided to be ready for the unexpected and to flex my style to co-create the change.

My experience is that *conversations create awareness*.

*

Facilitation has even saved me from conducting a disastrous behaviour change workshop. One morning of 2005, I was in the training room of a leading Financial KPO. I was all set to start my workshop on assertiveness. I thought that I had mastered it. What added to my excitement was the presence of four participants from Shanghai. Twenty minutes into the workshop, I knew I had not taken off well. As a trainer, I had conditioned myself to believe that the first 30 minutes are crucial. The ice breaker activity fizzled out with lukewarm energy. The tried and tested was not working for me that day. I was so wrapped up in my plan and excited about doing it right that I was oblivious to what was happening in the room.

The four participants from Shanghai had taken seats at the end of the room. They hesitated to make eye contact with me. I tried to get their attention by asking questions. Their responses were courteous and minimal. That day I experienced the difference between knowing and doing. My knowledge of cross-cultural differences and what I knew about engaging people as a trainer were not working. As I look back, I see what was happening then. My trainer mode was keen to include the four participants at the cost of ignoring the other twenty. That day, I felt like I had not shown up well as a trainer. I made a conscious effort since then not to slip again.

"This approach is not working today," I then expressed openly. All the 25 pairs of eyes looked up at me. "What can we do this time that would benefit you?" I continued. The participants looked surprised and alert! I then asked, "How about getting into groups to come up with your workshop goals?" This trick worked in the next 30 minutes. The room came alive and buzzed with conversations in small groups. The four participants from Shanghai joined different groups. They looked energetic for the first time since that morning. I also noticed that they spoke limited English. Yet, they had no difficulty communicating with the others. I had made some assumptions earlier about their challenge with communicating in English. These assumptions had affected the workshop and me as a trainer. As a facilitator, it is important to *be non-judgemental and stay neutral*, the lesson was right here.

As the group continued, they brought out the practical challenges of cultural differences in virtual teams. By the end of the day, they had actions for both the teams to take back. The best part was that the group gave feedback that both teams need to go through my workshop together. That was the best outcome for me and an unexpected one! I am glad that I had let go of the trainer in me to allow a facilitator to emerge. I could wear only one hat at a time. I chose to be a facilitator. It was the first time I had resorted to facilitative training. The challenge of engaging the group got me to leverage the group's wisdom. From that day, the way I designed workshops changed. I stepped into the world of facilitative training and entrepreneurship. I started my own people-development company soon.

❋

In my professional life, I play various avatars. I started as a behavioural trainer, then I became a change coach. I started using facilitation in training programs. I learned to create space: physical, mental, emotional, or spiritual for groups. The preparation with a clear objective in mind has helped me be flexible.

Since 2009, as a coach, I have used facilitation with groups. One change that I've noticed is that I moved away from giving suggestions and instructions. I stepped out of my comfort zone of using a slideshow. I experimented with music, movement, yoga, props, food, and indoor games. My focus shifted from downloading information to supporting the group in gaining insights. I started paying attention to the arrangements in the physical environment. It helped reduce barriers to move and interact. I experimented with walks in pairs on the lawn to sitting by the water fountain to reflect and share. The shy individuals opened easily away from the office. Participants felt that they were able to relax and stretch their minds to think differently. The open, physical space and the sound of water flowing gave a sense of privacy for discussions. I have also been experimenting with arranging the physical space in different ways. I have seen and experienced creative ways of using physical space at various facilitation learning events and conferences. I have picked up new ways and have used them too. My realisation is that *being open and flexible has helped me.*

*

A Small & Medium Manufacturing Company wanted to run an assessment center for its high potential managers. We had three rounds of discussions with the Managing Director (MD) before signing the contract. The first step was to facilitate conversations amongst the senior management team. The generic competencies for the organization were listed out using a facilitation process. We moved to identify high potentials. During the cross-functional discussion to identify high-potential managers, something surprised us. We saw the MD communicate in his autocratic style. Many times, the conversation was one way. A few function heads continued to agree to what he said. Other heads of functions were avoiding these discussion meetings. The group dynamics were not conducive to open discussions. We could not have moved forward. Finally, we realized that the MD had pre-decided who would make it to the high potential list. The entire exercise seemed futile.

Although late, we knew that we had missed out on having discussions with other stakeholders. In my excitement to bag the project, we had rushed into contracting, based on inputs of the MD. The other leaders were not engaged sufficiently. As a facilitator, my dilemma was that, if I had continued, it would have meant not valuing the others in the group. How would I then remain neutral in this situation? After a candid conversation with the MD, we decided to quit the project and part ways.

How could I have averted this situation? I learned that the intention of facilitation needs clarity. It is critical to have stakeholder conversations before contracting. Only focussing on the facilitation process is not enough. Group process facilitation requires pre-work and careful understanding. I realized that facilitation might seem like an ideal approach most times. It may not be the best always. This experience has made me aware that I need to focus on contracting and working norms. Using a process to get an alignment of expectations of the group can also help. I learned this the hard way. My lesson has been to *learn from my mistakes*.

In fact, my facilitation learning took a fast track in 2015. I joined the International Association of Facilitators (IAF) as a volunteer to organize the Asia IAF conference in Mumbai. I absorbed a lot from participating in facilitated strategy-meets-brainstorms, and conference calls. I started observing the style of each seasoned Indian and International facilitator. I have noticed the nuances of facilitation. Their pauses, an invitation to explore something, listening, asking powerful questions, and how they were present to the group. They managed the process by being invisible to the room. Above all, they were vulnerable as a human being. I learned so much by keeping my eyes and ears open.

A 3-day workshop facilitated by two certified professional facilitators introduced me to the fundamentals of facilitation. I now knew that a process included both generating different ideas (divergence) and narrowing them down (convergence). I understood the practical nuances of facilitating a group. Working with a group requires strong social contracting is what I realized. I created new processes and modified existing ones as required. I was now confident about using different facilitation processes appropriately.

Being a part of the India core committee as the Mumbai hub lead, from 2018 to 2020, brought some invaluable lessons. One lesson was knowing when to and when not to use facilitation. The other was how to strike a balance using facilitation. As leaders, we can probably hold that space and invite the team to explore.

I stepped forward to participate in a 3D Lab (it is a format for practicing facilitation and getting feedback on the competencies of a facilitator; 3D stands for Design, Develop & Deliver) in February 2019. The experience of designing the 90-minute session, brainstorming with the mentors, preparing for facilitation, keeping in mind the competencies made me confident. I decided to focus on my presence and neutrality during this session. In doing so, I missed out on setting a clear context. The self-reflection that followed helped me assess my abilities. The feedback from the certified professional facilitators was crisp and focussed on the competencies. My understanding of facilitation deepened.

When submitting my proposals for the All India IAF Annual Conference, I realized the importance of documenting each step of my design in detail. It helped me to be specific about the 'why's and the 'how's of my process. I got clarity on how I could flex as required. Documenting my design and going over it several times works for me. My submission is that *being part of a learning community is a blessing.*

*

In the past 26 years, as a member of an international social organization for women, I have been able to enrich my facilitation skills. In a voluntary organization, facilitation works wonders. As the president of the club for two terms, I have often resorted to using facilitation. To increase the engagement in the club, we identified a project where our contribution was not in funds but through our time. It was a new thing for all of us.

On the first Saturday of July, we went to the shelter that we had identified for a unique project. We had open conversations with the girls at a missionary school in small groups. These conversations gave us an idea of what the girls wanted to know and learn. These conversations worked magic on the club members, and they formed small teams of threes and fours. Each team took up one month and visited the school and executed the skill-building sessions. The project was soon on autopilot. More and more members started accompanying others. The bond between the members improved. They felt that they were indeed making a valuable contribution. The best part was that we did not spend anything from the club funds. Members took it upon themselves to fund the activities and organized donations for a mega annual event. It was a proud moment for me to present this unique project. My biggest take away from this was, when you let go of control as a leader, many leaders emerge. If not for using a facilitative approach, we would not have been able to touch those lives in this way. My insight: *trusting the power of the group works.*

*

Lastly, co-facilitating sessions is challenging. It has helped me evolve further and work on my facilitation mindset. I must admit that every time I see a new path in my facilitation journey, it seems like an uphill task. The journey is a long one. I feel the need to speed up before my time is up. It is an exciting journey full of bends, blind turns, challenges, creativity, and that is what keeps me going. I feel I am growing as a person.

At present, I conduct facilitative training sessions for corporates and industry bodies. I have facilitated and co-facilitated conversations for family-owned businesses, I work with millennial entrepreneurs. Working with women leaders is close to my heart. Moving to virtual facilitation has been an exciting transition. This world is exciting as there is still loads for me to explore here. My reality is that *I continue to learn and unlearn.*

Sharing my journey with you has brought back so many memories. It has reinforced my learnings and has furthered my resolve to keep moving forward on this journey. The more I do, the more I learn.

As I get ready to facilitate another virtual session now, I will continue to try, fall, get up to grow.

Facilitation to the Rescue!

Varsha Chitnis

Why had I taken a 5 AM flight to Chennai that morning? Let me tell you. An IT MNC was undergoing a global restructuring exercise. It resulted in several verticals getting consolidated and role redundancies. The Indian operations were to layoff close to 400 employees in a single day. My assignment was to prepare the Leadership to manage this unfortunate layoff. The leadership team needed to be ready to notify 400 people across cities in India. It was a grave situation, and the need for confidentiality was ver high. It explained my early morning flight and almost 'secret agent-like' back door entry to that state-of-the-art room. It was a first-time situation for the India operations, and they were not expecting it. They did not know how the leadership team might take it.

The leaders started walking in just before 8.AM. The MD was one of the first to arrive and shared, "Varsha, I am nervous, we've never done anything like this before. How do I tell people to leave just like that? Many of them have been recruited by me when we started here with just 50 people. I feel terrible right now". I fully realized the true nature of this assignment at that moment.

The MD and HR team shared the global decision and the impact on the India operations with the entire group. There was an uneasy quietness in the room. The air in the room was indeed heavy. I became aware that the emotional state of the leadership team was on a precipice; I realised I would need to be flexible to change my approach.

The team had a lot of questions on the layoff. It was necessary to get those questions some attention first. On a wall, I created a space called the 'The Parking Lot', where the leaders would put up all their questions. I discarded the idea of social contracting as it was an 'unusual situation'. Each leader shared the one thing that would support them to work in this group that day. These became the agreed group norms. It was now time to address the elephant in the room.

This group needed time to deal with their emotional state first. I set aside my plan for the day and invited these leaders to have conversations about their emotions at that time. Some spoke in pairs and the others in small groups. These exchanges created a feeling of being in it together. I gingerly stepped forward to check if they were ready to move ahead.

Next, the groups moved to identify the cause of these emotions. Amid this chaos, the head of legal compliance suddenly took a chair and sat down in the center with his eyes closed. As the others noticed this, the room suddenly became quiet again. He said, 'My biggest concern is 'What if I am the one asked to go?"' The silence that followed was deafening.

One leader who had joined the organization 18 months ago came forward and said, "It is possible? I am here because I was impacted in this manner last year." Another leader shared what she was thinking. Slowly, a conversation followed. Many leaders just chose to listen. They were communicating again. They resolved that they were in it together. They also decided to do what they could. What emerged was indeed powerful. The group was feeling connected in this time of crisis. This became possible because of the facilitated conversations. The group had diverged when sharing multiple emotions and slowly through these discussions they had converged to a point where they recognised their common emotions.

One group insisted that they discuss the adverse impact of the layoff. As a facilitator I checked with the entire team. A new process was introduced to enable this discussion. The leaders drew up a list and made several categories like financial, emotional, social impact and many others. This list related to the outplaced and retained employees. I was conscious of harnessing the group wisdom. The following step was to brainstorm regarding possible support to make the separation of these employees easier. It was not planned and came out that day in the moment as an outcome. The team felt satisfied that they had done something of value that day. The focus shifted to what they could do for the impacted employees. It changed the energy in the room. Empathy had replaced the anxiety in that room.

During lunch, the MD came over and said, "I am glad we dealt with ourselves. What's next?"

For the next hour, the room buzzed with activity. They formed new groups. Each group took some charts with the concerns shared in the morning. The HR team handed out copies of a detailed document specially designed for them. This document contained the details of the process for the layoff. I noticed, they made notes. The leadership got engrossed with understanding the process and started clarifying with one another. They were moving into getting ready to act on the day of the layoff.

I ask you, how would the group have received this information had it been shared in the morning? Changing the process to adapt to the emotional current in that room, had made a difference. The processes chosen had made it possible for all of them to speak out. By giving the leaders space and time, facilitation had helped them to move from a state of anxiety to empathy. They were able to bring back their focus to what they needed to do and get ready to act.

The notification happened a week later. I was present in the corporate office, where 185 employees had lost their jobs. All the leaders were in different locations overseeing the process in the best possible way. Facilitation had enabled the leaders to take complete ownership of executing this challenging task. It was a big thing. The leaders had proved their preparedness and much more that day! Facilitation had made this possible!

Dr. Shubha Rajan

Dr. Shubha Rajan is a people engagement professional, storyteller, trainer, counsellor, coach, mentor, and facilitator with over 30 years of work experience. She is the go-to person for aspiring trainers and facilitators for engaging methodologies and sessions scripting. She works with anyone wanting to take people development as a career. Her carefree countenance and careful attitude promise approachability and empathy. She believes in the platinum rule and so treats people the way they want to be treated.

'Facilitatee 2 Facilitator'

Shubha Rajan

I am reminded of the story 'The Cracked Pot' by Dulce Rodrigues from my childhood where a gardener used to hang two pots on a stick and carry water in them from the river to his mistress' house to water the plants. One pot had a little hole so by the time he reached the house it would be half empty. The other pot was robust, and the water filled in it would be intact.

One day, the pot with the hole said that it was feeling sad for the gardener. The pot was upset about its disability and therefore its disservice to the gardener. This was the holed pot's perspective. The other pot gave its counter perspective that the gardener must be very fond of the holed pot and that is why he was not replacing it. So, the gardener told both the pots that he was happy that he got one full pot of water. In order to make it easy for him to water the plants that he had planted on the pathway, he was still using the pot with the hole. The hole in the pot helped to water the plants on the way. Perspectives facilitated.

These two words have always been teasing me. Perspective and Facilitation. However, one point in their favour is that they both have taught me a lot and have helped me work towards experiencing facilitation as a way of life. What is a perspective? And what is Facilitation?

Perspective: (noun) (VIEW) A particular way of viewing things that depends on one's experience and personality. Perspective also means the ability to consider things in relation to one another accurately and fairly [**Cambridge Dictionary**]

Facilitation: Use the noun facilitation to describe helping, improving, or making something easier. The Latin word for "easy" is *facilis*. You can see this origin in *facilitation*, which means "the act of making something easier." [**Vocabulary.com**]

The relationship between the two: A perspective can lead to a vulnerable situation requiring facilitation. A facilitative process can in itself lead to multiple perspectives for the facilitated.

I think that I have been closely associated with these words from as far back as I can remember. I have chosen instances here in which I have been a 'facilitatee' and a facilitator.

Toddler meets with the Cops! | Facilitatee

I was around 3 years old when I got lost walking back home from my brother's friend's house. I took a wrong turn in the colony streets, in a small town called Durgapur in West Bengal. I turned into the 15th instead of the 13th. I reached the point in the street where my house should have been and found that it had moved. This was a police station.

There was a little ledge and after the long walk, I sat down, tired and hungry. It was already noon and the constable who was going for his lunch saw me there and asked me why I was sitting there in the sun and who was with me. I only knew English and Tamizh. He spoke in Bengali. Since I was not able to make sense to him, he took me inside and hoisted me up on the Inspector's table. The Inspector came around to me and the first thing he asked me, *"Bangla jano?"* (do you know Bengali)? I shook my head in the negative. He then said, "English?" so I said "yes". He then asked me my name, father's name and then my address. I knew the names but did not know the correct postal address of my house. He then asked me if I was hungry, I affirmed. He got me a huge glass of milk and a packet of biscuits. He held my glass of milk for me and fed me the biscuits till I polished them all off. He then took out the cycle, put me on the baby seat on the front bar and walked me down the streets to find my house.

Meanwhile, my father had come home for lunch. On hearing about me, he along with his colleague and the driver took his jeep and started searching for me. We met halfway. The cop handed me over to my father without a word. He only wanted my father to go to the police station and sign in a register. My father refused. In his conservative upbringing, entering a police station was a NO. That was his perspective. Kudos to my father's friend who bonded with the cop – he walked into the station, pulled out the register, made his entries in it, brought it out to the road near the jeep and told my father to sign it which my father did. A few takeaways to understand:

1. This should not have happened in the first place, however since it did, the policeman was very empathetic to my situation. He thought on his feet and quickly got me some food to keep me going. He empathized with the situation of a three-year-old.

2. Signing of a register was a non-issue but my father's upbringing came in the way. Perspective holder.

3. If the Inspector too had held on to his rule book, then I would have had to be put up for adoption later. He facilitated this issue because he was more worried for me, the victim, rather than his victory.

4. My father's friend was the savior for the day and the news carrier who came later in the evening and teased my father about it and told my mother the whole story. Otherwise we may never have known this side to my father. Truth will get known.

Plan B always works! (Plan A is vulnerable to failure) | Facilitatee

"Girls in our families do not dance on stage!" stated my father when I finished school and had wanted to join the classical dance school. My world came tumbling down my ears. I wanted to be a dancer, that was it. My ambition was to be a Bharatanatyam dancer, so I was quite shocked and stunned that suddenly this was a no entry. My small, ineffective protests were just that – ineffective. All I could do was sulk – there was no one to talk it through because we lived in a place called Asansol – a small town in West Bengal, and there was no one to reach out to. My father announced that he could allow me to go to Chennai and study further if I wanted, or else I could wait there, and he would get me married when I turned 21. The prospect of staying in Asansol with nothing to do for the next 5 years was the checkpoint.

It was December and I had until June of the next year to get to Chennai for the pre-university course. So, I travelled to Delhi to my aunt's place. My uncle facilitated the clarity that I was seeking. He debated that my father had a right to his perspective just as I had a right to mine.

Our life is controlled by perspectives – it is important to understand the perspective to move forward in life. He taught me to think out the various alternatives in a mind map fashion that my father had laid open for me though he had blocked one avenue – 1) I could study something else which meant I could stay in the city of Chennai in a hostel and learn independence, 2) I could study any academic subject of my choice, 3) My father had negated a career in dance but we had not talked about if it could continue to be a hobby. Every perspective has alternatives to it. Look for at least 3 alternatives to every perspective – yours, mine, and maybe a third agreeable one.

I came to Chennai and chose to do English, Psychology, and Economics. I did pass in the first class and made my father feel proud. It is prudent to seek opportunities to better yourself each time. Raise the bar and challenge the image in the mirror. Some lessons from this:

1. Everyone has a right to their perspective.
2. Every perspective will have many alternatives
3. Raise the bar and challenge the image in the mirror.
4. Adversity is also a hotbed of innovation.

Why me? | Facilitatee

Crossroads
Alice came to a fork in the road. 'Which road do I take?' she asked.
'Where do you want to go?' responded the Cheshire Cat.
'I don't know,' Alice answered.
'Then,' said the Cat, 'it doesn't matter. If you do not know where you are going, then any road with get you there.'

— **Lewis Carroll,** *Alice in Wonderland*

Life was at a huge, multilane crossroad, and I was Alice in Wonderland. I walked into the work world armed with a BA in English Literature, a doctoral degree in Defence and Strategic Studies and a Journalism certification in 1990. My education left me either overqualified or under qualified for most jobs. I had always sported a very carefree countenance though careful in attitude. I was willing to learn any number of skills along the way if that would help. I was a veritable square peg in a round hole that did not fit. Some of my perspectives:

1. Crossroads teach one to choose objectively
2. Change is circumstantial – square or round – every peg can be fitted into a hole with some customisation

Career footprint | Amateur Facilitator, unknowingly

My first proper job was at the American Consulate General as a librarian in the USEFI library. Sitting in that library and talking to all the young aspirants going to the USA for higher studies made me read up all the college catalogues and get familiar with the fee structure and the assistance programs.

As I worked there, I realized that a lot of youngsters had no clue what subject to choose, what to study, or what they wanted to do with their life. I learnt to interact with people, speak to the youngsters, even helped them make a decision on which colleges to narrow down to. Without any knowledge of any process, I was already using the 5Ws (Who, what, where, when, why) & 1H (how) continuously. They were to first list out the top 5 colleges of their preference, get them to diverge and converge using a 2x2 metrics which when opened out would resemble a rough fish bone theory. At the end, they would harvest their own thoughts and come up with workable choices and then start their application process. As it was a library there was a lot of stationery available and the students put all of that to good use. Those were the days of the microfilms which were small negatives that was inserted into a reading machine and it showed an entire educational institution in it. That taught me that 'less is more' and if the eyes can see, it the mind can take it in relevance to the requirement.

Some thoughts on my learnings here:

1. I was over-qualified for the job on hand but that need kept my ego intact

2. Your qualification could disqualify you for some things

3. If you have it in you to help others and simplify things for them then you will find various methods to facilitate. 5W 1H, 2×2 metrics, Fish bone analysis, affinity diagram, divergence and convergence.

4. Less is always more.

Goode Dag! (Good Day! in Dutch) | Facilitatee

I was interviewed by the Ambassador of the Royal Netherlands Embassy and then the vice consul took me to lunch to his home. Coming from the innards of Chennai with minimal exposure to any kind of richness, just entering the house was making me nervous. It was January and cold in New Delhi. At that time, I did not realise that this was an extension of the interview. I had nil cutlery skills and the table was laid out with all the required paraphernalia of a sit-down lunch, fine dining style. The soup was served, and I waited, hoping that the Vice Consul's wife would start and I would copy her. But she waited for me to start as I was the guest. In my hesitation, I looked around the room to calm myself and found their cook by my side with a water jug. He then told me in Hindi that I needed to start from the outer most instrument and work my way inwards (*bahar se andar tak*). So saying, he helped me with my napkin and left. After that it was a sail through.

I had come a long way from the conservative Chennai girl to being in the capital city as a single working woman! Cheerful in countenance and careful in attitude helped me a lot in New Delhi. I was there for three years and there were many instances of facilitation as I was the Indian go-to person for the Dutch people living there. I learnt the Dutch language so that I could communicate better with the expatriates.

1. Help can come from any quarter, look for it – a cook was able to recognize that I was not comfortable with cutlery. I may not have got the job if I had goofed up at the lunch.

2. Post this incident I learnt a lot of the finer skills as they were required in and on the job.

3. Soft is hard – consciously facilitate them, everyone needs it (soft skills are hard)

Back to the pavilion | Facilitator, formally

From the Embassy, it was back to Chennai. By now I realized that I was happy only when I was helping, developing, listening to and serving others. Therefore, I certified myself in Leadership and other training programs. I underwent the Effective Personal Productivity program by LMI, (Leadership Management International) of the LMI University, Texas, USA. The chief franchisee for India hired me and I was facilitating training programs for corporates.

LMI afforded me a lot of training practice, I was in charge of the Leadership program, the personal effectiveness program and the sales program. Apart from this, I was also helping to develop the franchisee base in all of India and working with the MECE principle – Mutually Exclusive and Collectively Exhaustive. To keep us all on the same page, I brought out a newsletter as well. In my facilitation sessions I was using a lot of tools, however the fact remained that it was content facilitation.

I realized that facilitation is a simple norm. Wanting to be available with anticipational, objective intelligence is all that is required. Facilitation is all about wanting to make anything easy for others who are finding it difficult. The source of information, knowledge and process skill are all there in our lives. As is often said, Life can only be understood backwards but it has to be lived forward. Lessons taken from the past always come in handy to put together solutions for the future. This was my base camp for learning facilitation.

Onwards to Consulting | Facilitator

The Consulting Group took me as a L&D professional with HR responsibilities as well. One of the projects I handled there was the plus two (+II) education syllabus for the state of Kerala. It was a comparative study of the Kerala state board education with other southern states, the other available Indian boards and the International Baccalaureate board as well. I was the lead for this study. It was a great challenge working with the state government's school teaching staff. As part of the information gathering, I needed to get teachers together in various schools, serve questionnaires and collect answers. They never came on time, many did not show up, there was a show of apathy. I was quite disheartened, but I remembered from my earlier experience that if I start something then I need to see it through to the end. I worked at getting maximum responses. First, I got the education secretary to announce that their daily allowance and travel would be taken care of by the Government of Kerala. Then I put out a WIIFM (What is in it for me?) poster with 2 points:

1. I needed help in understanding the current syllabus that they were following. I also mentioned that whoever came to the workshop would get to incorporate their thoughts into the new syllabus.

2. If they came, they would learn interesting methods of teaching with fun and excitement. No more boring books. A kind of quid pro quo.

Then the teachers came. I collated my comparison and brought out my new recommendations.

Towards this, I held many workshops at various districts and the first question they had to answer was what makes the students

SAD, MAD, or GLAD about their subjects. The next was to write out what made them 'sad', 'mad', or 'glad' about the syllabus that they were following. Both views were again mutually exclusive and collectively exhaustive. Once we got the converging needs from both the exercises, it was easy to marry the two needs and make a new syllabus by taking the exact requirement from the comparative study. All lacks were fulfilled, and the teachers felt a great sense of ownership to the new syllabus offered. Many teachers gave feedback that this learning had been great fun and they wanted the freedom to teach in this way. The Kerala state government's Education Secretary was surprised that so many teachers actually turned up for this exercise, as earlier this was not the norm. He also accepted the teachers' request to use interesting teaching methods. The one-point fallout from this was that he also asked the teachers to form groups based on their subjects and compile a set of interesting teaching methods so that there was documentation and reference material as well.

Some takeaways:

- Perspectives of the teachers:
  1. WIIIFM (What Is In It For Me?)
  2. Why put an effort for a nonstarter. What is going to come out of this anyway.
  3. Why is some other state consultant coming to work about our education system?
- Learning:
  1. Put out the WIIIFM clearly, there are no free lunches
  2. Keep your promise – I had promised them a good time, so I saw to it that they learnt some easy processes, had a good lunch, and enjoyed themselves.

3. They were like children, no pressure, pure learning fun.

4. SAD-MAD-GLAD and MECE (Mutually Exclusive Collectively Exhaustive) are good group processes when large crowds are involved. I had close to a hundred teachers each time.

5. When you are facilitative, others also become empowered to be facilitative.

IT! The coveted zone | Facilitator

IT was still a coveted zone. I came in a little late in my career to this arena as a design solutions manager. I started work with regular training. Then we got an initiative to work on. It seemed that clients were not able to communicate with the teams on the floor. The old order was a safe method. Every positional person met with his/her counterpart in the client organization. This took time. Speed was of essence. Clients started to want to meet the developer of the code directly and work with the teams. We realized the danger of letting our teams meet with the client team. Our teams did not have any consulting language or client-facing skills. A mandate was given to me from the business that I needed to cover around 25,000 employees in India in various locations in various levels with programs on consulting and client-facing skills in one year.

A team was put together and we designed a level-based program on the topic. Now the programs were ready, but we did not have that many facilitators to deliver these programs. I got to work and created a trainers' pool. My team floated flyers and messages that anyone who wanted to do their bit in giving back to the organization could join the trainer pool.

At first, there was no enthusiasm again because the WIIIFM (what is in it for me) was not addressed. Then, I put out a Reward and Recognition plan with no money involved. Employees and management were mutually happy. I did put in a caveat that every volunteer would be interviewed and only if found suitable would we be able to take them on board. I had around 1,500 employees from the mid-management and the senior management willing to go through this. My requirement was good and correct English language skills as the content was already available with me. We brought it down to 800 trainers who were selected for this feat. The data crunching experts put the calendars out for a 'train the trainer' program. Some of us travelled extensively and got trainers up to speed so that they could start delivery. The program had a lot of facilitative activities and the new trainers liked the fact that they do not need to know content/theory, they just need to carry out the activities and the processes and the participants would learn what we wanted them to. This was a sure shot to success. We covered more than the number required.

Key achievements:

1. We covered more than 25,000 in one year – that was the mandate

2. Client delight was the cream on the cake

3. We got invited to deliver programs at the client space for their employees

4. There was a training pool to stay

5. We took on other initiatives since we had the resources available across locations

6. The training unit became a business center from the earlier cost center status

Thus began my career as a librarian and I retired as a senior solutions manager last year.

The IAF

I joined the International Association of Facilitators in 2016 from the annual national conference in Bangalore. All that I already knew as methodologies in facilitation were validated and reiterated for me here in this space. The number of process, methods and tools to facilitate help in quickly sorting out the requirement are available, but the base requirement is a heart that wants to help make the tough easy. I am an active member of the IAF.

*

Being a facilitatee and facilitator are two parts of the same coin. We may choose to pay it forward or afterward, that is all. Facilitating when and wherever required enables peaceful co-existence. I continue to carry my cheerful countenance and careful attitude. I have repeated this a few times and you must be wondering why. A cheerful countenance makes for easy approachability. A careful attitude makes for a caring stance and people feel that they are being cared for when they come to me. I find both these very useful for me in my facilitative journey. Our characteristics and attitude need to add up to a harmonized picture which speaks of faith and trust. That trust is what makes people open up to me about their issues and perspectives. Perspectives are not in our control, but facilitation is.

I am POSH!

Shubha Rajan

If you have noticed, the synonyms of the word POSH are Aristocratic, Noble, Classy, High Class etc. I always thought of this word in these terms until I came to the work world and that too as late as 2008, when I learnt that POSH is the "Prevention of Sexual Harassment" in the workplace. I actually stumbled into it.

I had begun a new job in the IT sector as a senior advisory manager and was very busy as it was a new role in the project and the IT sector was new for me. I was a lateral hire to the job. I noticed that I was constantly being followed whenever I was in the common areas by another employee – loud talking, abrasive behaviour, finding reasons to come in front of me. I was being harassed by a manager at work because I had joined in the place where he had wanted his candidate to come. He was not on my project but was constantly finding reasons to come on to my project floor. He would pass by my desk making loud comments on my gender, on my being a doctorate, other things like dress, age etc. I was ignoring all this for some time because I was new and I wasn't sure how I could possibly complain. But slowly, I started hearing complaints from other women colleagues as well about this manager. Whenever something wasn't done according to him, he would start harassing his female colleagues. Then, I took it up to the diversity leader and spoke to her about it. There was no diversity leader in Chennai at that time so I offered to take that role as a give back to the organisation. I also offered to facilitate the whole situation to closure. The man was quite senior, so we had to be very careful and circumspect in our actions.

Since all the other women employees were in junior positions, I took the lead. I set up a meeting with the diversity leader and the women who were willing to file a complaint about this manager. After the initial purging of complaints, we needed to form an action plan. Looking at the seniority of the manager I did not want to take any brash steps. At that time, I was not aware of the POSH (Prevention of Sexual Harassment) liability of an organisation or that it was a serious issue. I thought to myself that if a man is displaying his sense of power through harassment, then he must either be idle and having too much time or he must be carrying some emotional baggage.

The organisation helped by constantly pointing out that there was zero tolerance to POSH. That made it easier for me to plan. We wanted to first teach him and a few of his colleagues the meaning of working with colleagues of the opposite gender. It was around the time that the Women's Day was coming up. However, we decided that we needed to be careful and so we brainstormed to find a solution. We hit upon a plan and got a couple of managers from each project to bring in their wives for the celebration. We also got some women managers to bring in their husbands for the show. We took pains to facilitate his wife to come in for the program because this whole show was to get the message across that harassment would not be tolerated. Under the pretext of doing many skits on behaviour we called the spouses and collected information about the employee at home. We learned that this manager was by nature very dominant and quite a loud and angry person.

The half day program had lunch and some music & dance programs and then drama. So in the skit that we did, we got his behaviour depicted very well. His wife innocently enjoyed the skit and even congratulated the actors. I purposefully followed a bit of psychodrama and multiple intelligence to get the message across. Each skit was played out with a need for the audience to recognise the behaviour of a particular manager. After a series of these skits we also showed the consequences of what this kind of behaviour could bring about to one's career. Humiliation, ostracization, no promotion, negative publicity or even loss of job were some of the repercussions based on the intensity of the harassment. The resultant messaging was very powerful and from the next day, there was a perceivable change in a lot of people's behaviour at the work.

The other feather in our cap was that I was announced as the Gender, Diversity and POSH leader for the location – a position that I held until I retired last year. We also got a quick helpline called "MITR" for anyone who needed to file in a complaint or even just talk it out to someone else. As head of the Learning function I also got a POSH session included in the induction program for new hires. The organisation also insisted that every employee undergo an online course and get certified every year. This was another drive that I was responsible for. I have had numerous instances to deal with that has built my objectivity. Therefore, my perspectives on this subject are very clear, my investigations are always objective to the issue and not the person, and my judgements are always fair to the victim and the victor equally.

Even today, I continue to work as an external advisor-member, deliver training to organisations on the subject, help investigate cases, facilitate understanding, volunteer to coach, mentor and counsel victims who have been subjected to POSH and suffer trauma.

I have noticed that parenting is a key input here. If boys are treated with objectivity and wisdom through their development years then they are likely to be more affable to the opposite gender in their lives, be it at home or the workplace. If girls are taught to value themselves better instead of a "I am equal to a man" syndrome they are also better able to appreciate the men in their lives.

A healthy appreciation of each other can go a long way in creating a POSH-free ecosystem that is safe for all.

I am a POSH trainer, and I say it with a heavy heart.

Arvind Murwaha

Arvind is a highly experienced business transformation coach and talent development expert with more than three decades years of experience across various industries. He has helped many large-sized companies globally and start-ups to build their talent capabilities and organization cultures that support business success. He is the CEO and Coach at CRESKO Consulting, a premium Business Transformation and Leadership Development solution provider. As a Leadership Coach and Talent Transformation consultant, he has been instrumental in enabling results for organization across a wide range of industries.

The Experiential Facilitator

Arvind Murwaha

*"We learn from Life. It's a hard journey.
It's a rewarding journey."*

Learning through our own experiences is good. Learning from other people's experiences is smarter! A large part of my learning has been through a wide array of experiences. Some by choice, some unintended. These experiences have defined me as a facilitator of positive change – for businesses and for leaders.

I started my working career as a design engineer, but soon discovered that I actually did not want to be that. My journey from a design engineer to a facilitator of change has been about moving away from what I did not want. It was about experiences that helped me discover and refine the facilitator within. And while I did not know it then, there was a need for practicing facilitation in all the jobs that I ever did. Had I realised the benefits of *facilitation* right at the start of my career, I would have made much better progress and got much better results. It does not matter what your profession is. You could be in business operations or sales or HR. Facilitative approach will make a huge difference in what you are able to get done in your work and your life.

Getting Others to Agree

The initial ten years of my career were in various business roles. Operations, supply and distribution, maintenance and even fire &

safety. My success early on was due to the fact that I could work well with people. Connecting with them and getting work out of them. Then I started using authority and rules to get work done.

And that was where it all started to go wrong. I discovered that being friendly and approachable was a better option. That way, I could get more work done rather than by being authoritative. This built the foundation layer for me to become a facilitative leader.

The attribute of being good in dealing with people opened up the opportunity of a sales job for me. I thought that my success in sales would come from being a strong personality – someone who could talk others into deals and get the orders. How wrong I was! Experience taught me that a forceful selling style does not work. When I was trying to convince, I would force my ideas on the customers. And that would often fail. Getting people to agree was not about forcing them into agreement!

I had to learn the hard way that the sales process started from listening to the needs of the customer. I had to learn to ask questions and listen to what the customer says. What worked was asking the right questions. Questions that helped customers make the right choices. This ability to ask questions has taken years to refine. The journey had started. This was another brick put in place in the making of a facilitative leader. Ability to frame and ask the right questions is key to being a good facilitator.

Human Interaction, Not Numbers

Even as I succeeded in the sales job, I was not that happy with it. Was that what I wanted to do all my life? The question "Who am I?" did not seem to get answered. I was someone who liked to interact with people, who liked to help people. What would excite me is the connection I created with people and not the sales numbers that I would deliver. I cherished the respect people gave because of the help I would give. No one appreciated the "push" I gave to increase sales. They always remembered me as the friendly face who listened to them. For me, the exciting part of the sales job was that I could connect with many people.

In fact, the most satisfying part of the job for me was coaching someone in how to sell and how to succeed. And the interesting part of coaching for me was that it required me to understand the other person. At first, I made several mistakes while coaching. Because I would often "tell" them what they should do. I thought as a coach, that was my job. What I did not realise was that nothing I could tell the other person would solve their challenges. What would work for them, would be the solution they would come up for themselves. My job as a coach was to "facilitate" their thinking process. That is something I learnt the hard way through experience. Failure was a guiding light for me. Change was a great panacea to my pains as a coach and a sales leader.

"Facilitation is a human thing."

As a manager or a coach or a trainer, we have to do some tasks, plan for execution and take some structured actions. What we need to realise is that these are the tools. Tools to get work done in the most effective manner. We need to use these tools in a "facilitative" manner. Use them to help people in our teams to think and arrive at better decisions. Facilitation is about catering to the "human" dimension. About how people will be able to process their ideas and arrive at conclusions.

Understanding human behaviour and its impact on results became a passion for me. And this guided my journey further towards professional development as a facilitator.

The Experiential Facilitator

There are occasions in life when you have someone who indicates a direction for you. And it changes the path you take. One of my mentors did that for me when he sent me to a Train-The-Trainer program at Cape Town, South Africa. This was a very comprehensive program. Its purpose was to make business managers become training leaders. It made me fall in love with how we can help people learn. For a long time, I have held a belief: when you do what you like to do, you may or may not succeed, but when you do what you love to do you will excel. So, I made a decision to change my line of work. I got certified on a host of programs and tools. Eventually, I moved away from being a head of sales to take up the role of a head of the Learning & Development function.

In an attempt to help people learn, I dug deeper into adult learning principles. Trying to understand what helped adults learn and change. To me it emerged that "teaching" is not something that works with adults. They will learn themselves through what they experience. The main task was to get them interested in learning and bringing about a change. We have to help people realise that they will benefit from change. Then, help them figure out what change they need to make and how to make it. This was turning out to be a bit of a challenge for me.

I got exposed to a facilitative way of making learning happen through a very interesting experience. At that time, I was working for a multinational oil company. The top executive team had a lot of conflict going on amongst them. Our managing director, thus, talked to a senior facilitator at our Singapore office. He would run a session on team alignment for our top team. I had to coordinate to make sure the execution was smooth. So I connected with this senior facilitator in Singapore. The idea was to understand from him what would he need for the program. He said that there would be no need for a slide projector, there would be no sharing of content. Now that to me was a shock. How can you do a training program without a slideshow? He then asked me to get flip-charts, thick sketch pens of different colours, crayons and a lot many post-it slips. Now this excited me, but it was still very confusing. My managing director reassured me. He said that this facilitator was very experienced and knew what he was doing.

Long story short, the session was very successful. There was no team building model that the trainer shared. There was no content about how team alignment should happen. There were only three group exercises. One, to explore what the current challenges were in the team; second, to explore the desired state; and the third, for coming up with actions to get to that desired state. The participants themselves created a better way of functioning in the organisation. This would enable conflicts to get managed in a more effective manner. It was amazing. It was very deep learning for me. It was the start of a journey to discover "facilitation" in its true form for me.

I then experimented with this style of *facilitated learning* myself. One of the first programs I used to conduct was a 5-day Sales Excellence Program. This was for experienced sales managers. In the beginning, when I would be delivering content, I would be a vociferous trainer. The forceful personality of the trainer in me would come out. I would deliver with "high impact" so that the learners take note. People liked it and at the end of the session would give very good feedback. Everyone would be happy. Yet, it did not help in their learning. Often the participants would say, "Well, what you are saying is right, but it will not work for me." Have we not all heard this from the participants of our learning sessions?

Then, I switched to the facilitative style. I used various group exercises followed by proper debriefs. I stopped being the forceful trainer. I would be there to let the learners themselves uncover the learning points. This switch was very difficult to make.

At first, it appeared to me that these exercises were "games". Some sort of fillers to energise the learners. Finally, I realised that the real learning happened during these "group experiences". When executed well, they were not mere exercises. They were actually processes that help people think, express and generate ideas. It helped them deliberate on their ideas and decide what to do with them. Facilitating sales excellence became my forte due to this. 'Selling Value: facilitating Sales Excellence' became one of my successful flagship programs.

> *"Facilitative learning is about enabling people to go through their learning journey."*

Experiences like these also taught me something important. I realised that the learning process for people started much before the session. It started from their realisation of their learning need. In some way, they have to be "facilitated" to uncover their need for learning. In fact, most of the times it is their seniors who have to be "facilitated" to identify the correct needs. I have come across CEOs who tell me that their leaders need to learn to communicate better. The CEO would say that his leaders are not able to influence their peers, leading to conflicts. A careful questioning soon reveals that the need actually is for goal alignment in the top team. Once there is a proper goal alignment, they tend to listen more to each another. The communication becomes smoother.

Facilitator by Design

At first, I was not inducted formally to the world of facilitation. A lot of my learning was self-driven. And yes, you can learn a lot about facilitation once you set your mind to it.

I started with an understanding of the functioning of the mind and thinking processes. These principles explain how an adult's decision-making process works – and it's about any decision people have to make. Decisions about how to solve a problem, decisions about who will do what, decisions about how to run a business – any and all such decisions. And the decision made by an individual himself/herself is the only decision they will ever abide by. Decisions made by others are not given the highest priority. People give more importance to what they themselves think and uncover. The key is to let people think and decide for themselves.

Something that helped me apply the power of facilitation is what I call the 'Ask-Tell Spectrum'. In business situations, there are occasions when people have to be "told" to do what they have to do. And yet, people think better when we pose questions to them. So when do we exercise the Tell mode and when do we employ the Ask mode? The Ask-Tell spectrum answers that question. And here is how I have found it can be understood clearly.

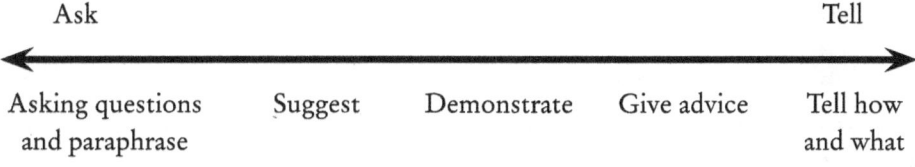

What I learnt was that when you want people to think and decide, asking the right questions worked best. The more you are able remain on the "Ask side" of this spectrum, the more effective you are as a people leader. This led me to start changing my people-leading style. In corporate meetings and learning sessions I moved to more of the facilitative mode. It was liberating to let the group wisdom evolve on its own.

Let me share how facilitation worked for me outside of the training room. There is always a pressure from the business to do the training in one day or half a day. And learning takes more time. I tried convincing the business leaders about the need for a longer duration of training programs. It did not work. And then I realised, I was trying to impose my beliefs on the business managers. Being facilitative would work better in aiding the business leaders' thought process. Help them identify what change they needed. And then help them become aware of how much time would they be ready to invest if the change was to actually happen.

This gave me good results. From approval of L&D budgets to mutual agreement on calendarized programs. The main task was to get leadership decide on the priority given to training. The key was to link the performance of leaders with the training and development of their teams. Then, my challenges of getting people interested in attending programs reduced. Not just because the programs were better – of course they were of high quality. But because the business leadership had decided to give priority to learning. Priority for investment in time and resources for learning. It was their decision and hence they implemented it!

Another thing that helped me on my journey was getting certified as an executive coach. I got this certification through the International Coaching Federation (ICF). Executive coaching involves techniques for one-on-one facilitation. It involves building trust and rapport. It involves the practice of framing and asking questions effectively. It involves facilitative techniques to help the leader being coached to gain insights. Once a COO asked me to coach a leader to be less aggressive and more responsive to his peers. His expectation was that I would meet the leader once and convince him to change. I went about asking some questions to the COO like what was the negative impact of the aggression on part of the concerned leader? How was the business getting affected? How much time investment would be worth if the leader was able to actually change? We agreed on six coaching sessions and one online assessment to be done. I created and used an EVOLVE coaching process. The resultant change was very much visible. I have been using the EVOLVE Coaching System to coach leaders for the past many years now. It has helped me practice the art and science of facilitated coaching to help them gain insights.

The Ever-Changing Facilitator

So what changed for me to transform myself into an effective facilitator?

The first change was my approach. I stopped *telling* people about what they need and shifted to letting people uncover their own learning needs. Left to themselves, they would not do it. There was a need to "facilitate" their thinking. A lot of times I would go with a pre-determined agenda: they have to decide on 'this' need. I changed this approach to say: "They will identify what will help them succeed". Whatever their learning needs may be as per them, it has to be taken care of. It's their learning process. Without self-realisation, they will never uncover their real developmental need.

Another change was about a change in the learning environment. Changing it to make it more conducive to learning. Not only the physical environment – which too underwent a change – but more critical was the mental state in which participants would learn. Is it a safe environment? Does it provide for free expression? Would it provide for hearing of divergent views without judgement? Would the group be able to deliberate on ideas without someone taking over a dominant role? We have to take care of all these and more aspects like these, which I learnt eventually the hard way.

I had to change the design of the learning sessions as well. I had to move away from simple content download sessions. I designed exercises that would enable participants to uncover their learning points. I had to learn to run facilitation processes for self-discovery, processes to enable self-reflection, and group facilitation processes to enable group wisdom to emerge.

In 2012, I was to do a leadership program for an Indian promoter-led company. They had business in India and the US. They were expanding very fast. Their leaders needed value addition to their leadership skills. Now how do you teach senior leaders with 30–40 years of business experience? And the answer is you cannot teach. You can help them learn. So I designed a 3-day 'Managing For Results' program. It addressed aspects of managing the self, managing relationships, and managing business. The design was completely facilitative. The participants included the Managing Director and the CXO team of India. By the end of the program, each leader had created his and her own leadership growth roadmap. At the end of a session, one very senior leader said to me, "Thanks for coming into my life!" Now that to me was the high impact of facilitation that charges me up. I got a mandate to conduct that program across their organisation in India as well as in New York. And since then, 'Managing For Results' has been one of my flagship programs. The power of facilitation made this happen!

For me, facilitation has also worked for business meetings and problem-solving scenarios. In one of my assignments, the HR team across the country was coming together for a conference. It was an annual review and action-planning session for becoming more effective as HR. There would be 75 HR managers and leaders in the conference and there was a debate how best to capture the group wisdom. I designed and facilitated a half-day session based on group facilitation processes. It enabled the HR group to deliberate on "from here to there" – from the current reality to the desired state. We were able to deliberate on the challenges, highlight the obstacles, debate on possible solutions, and ideate on the required actions. I used various facilitative processes like 'Conversation Cafe', 'Affinity', 'ORID', and 'Force Field analysis'. Two themes emerged in that workshop; themes that as an HR team they would work on, to transform the HR function. Two and a half hours, 75 HR leaders: all viewpoints expressed and deliberated on, and action plan created. It was the power of facilitation at play!

The Learning Facilitator

As I used the facilitation methods, I realised that there were some gaps. I had to equip myself with skills and tools that enabled better facilitation. An exposure to literature by established process facilitators helped. Facilitators like Thiagi, Keith McCandless and Henri Lipmanowicz. Some seniors guided me on facilitative approaches as well. It's always good to have a mentor who helps you understand how to adopt a facilitative approach. The literature and online material on asking questions helped. Framing questions is one of the critical parts of a facilitative process design.

Learning from experienced facilitators also helps. Some years back I experienced a very structured facilitative process. It was for problem-solving, facilitated by a colleague from Germany. This was an exercise on solving some serious design-related problems. Problems in design of machines that we were manufacturing. He conducted a two-day workshop completely based on facilitative processes to solve the challenges. He used Brainstorming, Conversation Cafe, Dot Voting, and Fish Bone Analysis. There are many structured processes that are available online to choose from. Sessions Lab is one good resource for exploring such processes.

Then, I got exposed to IAF – the International Association of Facilitators. What a great source of help for facilitators. I saw many experienced facilitators in action. And while I had experience and knew about facilitation, I did not hesitate in enrolling as a learner.

I became a member of IAF and could immediately access a massive library of processes as well as connect with a large group of experienced facilitators whom I could learn from. I got an opportunity to facilitate a session at the national conference in Delhi. Designing that session from scratch and doing it for a mature audience was a great experience. Some very different processes were used in their modified versions like Metaphors (Bridges, Magnets and Islands) and Lotus Blossom, which worked very well. Some of the experienced peers even shared feedback on how well it went.

Being open to learning has helped me become a better facilitator.

The Well-Equipped Facilitator

Many a times, people have asked me how to become an effective facilitator. It's a journey everyone has to take. Here, I share five things that have helped me equip myself:

1. Facilitator Mindset

Equipping myself with a facilitator's mindset has been the most critical aspect of being a facilitator. The word itself means to me that I "facilitate". Not directing the audience. No forced download of content. No forced learning. As a facilitator, I have to think of outcomes of a session that emerge from the group processes. For example, "Learn selling skills" is a training objective. "Explore best ways to sell" is a facilitative outcome.

2. Facilitator Skill-Set

Equipping myself with appropriate skills has helped. The International Association of Facilitators provides a well-documented set of facilitator competencies. Understanding these competencies and building them into your facilitative work will help.

3. Facilitator Tool-Kit

Building my own tool kit of processes, support materials and online tools. This has been an on-going exercise. The facilitative processes are available at the IAF site (library). Other sites like the Sessions Lab and Liberating Structures are also helpful.

4. Facilitator Experience

Experience has been a great help – my own experience and the experience of others. IAF provides a safe space to gain this insight. One can volunteer to run sessions. Taking part in learning labs helps. Attending sessions of experienced facilitators helps.

5. Facilitator Mentor

Sometimes, we get overwhelmed with an information overload. Sometimes, there is minimal help available. Taking on an experienced facilitator as a mentor will benefit a lot. It will smoothen the journey and shorten the learning span.

In the end, I would say, learning through experiences has worked for me. These experiences have shaped my growth as a professional.

Being the Experiential Facilitator has been a wonderful journey!!

Facilitating Results

Arvind Murwaha

A wintry night of Delhi. Evening bonfire at a farmhouse. Sixteen leaders of a global automotive company huddled together around the fire to create their future. That's where I found myself in February a few years back.

It all started when a multinational automotive company approached me to run a leadership development workshop. Their need was to groom the General Managers heading their dealerships so that they could be more effective leaders and grow the business. The audience – primarily consisting of the General Managers of their dealerships – were very experienced salespeople but now they needed to hone their leadership skills to become more effective business leaders for their respective units. Honestly, when I got this assignment, I had no experience in the automotive industry. Yet, conducting a leadership workshop was going to be a cake walk, as that's what I had been doing for more than a decade. At least that's what I'd thought. But how wrong I was!

One of the expectations set by the company was growth in sales numbers. The leaders were to create an action plan of how they would grow their business. Since I was not an expert on the automotive market, it would not have been possible for me to *tell* them how to do it. I did not know how things actually worked in the automotive business or how the car dealerships made money. Yes, I could help them become better leaders. But how to sell more cars? That was not my domain knowledge. It soon became a challenging assignment. So I resorted to the use of facilitative techniques and processes.

Designing and preparing the facilitative workshop took considerable time. The first step was to get them to open up their thinking process – to create a non-threatening, open environment. An environment that would encourage a free exchange of ideas, an environment in which all the participating leaders were actively engaged.

We would use group processes to generate and exchange ideas. First, there was a need to create divergent ideas. Ideas that would go beyond the normal. Ideas that may not get an expression through usual logical thinking. For this, I used the "conversion caffe" process. This process enables un-hindered conversations in small groups.

The conversations would be around specific questions framed for the leaders. Each leader would get a chance to express themselves, even using charts to capture all the ideas. The leaders then viewed the thoughts and ideas generated by each group, for which we used the 'gallery walk'. We also used a "force field" analysis to identify what factors supported the business and what acted as the obstacles. This enabled the capturing of a collective wisdom.

I then led the leaders into identifying areas that they thought needed to be explored further: problem areas that needed practical solutions for the growth of the business. Identification and prioritisation of such areas was done through the 'dot voting' activity.

The next step was for the leaders to create solutions for the problem areas they had identified. In small groups they created ideas through a process known as the 'lotus blossom'. In this process they first take a problem area and place it in the centre of a flip chart. The participants then generate ideas to solve that problem – like the petals of a lotus flower around the centre of the flower. Once this was done, the flip charts were rotated amongst the smaller groups so that every participant could add to the ideas for overcoming each problem area.

Then, the group was divided into triads. In each triad, one person would talk about their challenges; they would choose which of the ideas generated earlier would help in their opinion. The other two would act as consultants to the first person. Their role would be to act as sounding boards – listen to the person who was sharing and give appropriate suggestions about their selection of ideas and solutions. Then, the roles would change. Thus, each person would got the opportunity to get a "consult" from the others.

Each leader would then create an individual action plan. For this, they used a 'Stop-Start-Continue' process. What would they stop doing? What would they start doing? And finally, identify what was working well so that they could continue doing it. These action plans were then detailed to make them practical and implementable. What, when, who and other such elements would also get added to make the action plans more comprehensive.

Undoubtedly, all this work took time. The session got extended right into the late evening. The participants decided to convene even after dinner. They were able to see practical solutions to their business issues. This excited them and they wanted to complete the exercise.

Throughout the workshop, my role had been that of a facilitator. I did not share any 'business model'. I did not share any content knowledge – I could not. What did I do instead? I created a safe space for the expression of thoughts. I formulated specific questions that would lead to solutions. I facilitated group processes for enabling leaders to generate ideas and find solutions; benefiting from the collective wisdom of their peers.

For me, what was heartening to see was the level of engagement that was generated. These facilitative methods helped create an environment of free exchange of ideas. There was a lot of passion at display. There was a collaborative environment where everyone contributed to everyone. It highlighted the axiom 'all of us together are much more than just the sum of all of us.'

Naturally, the results were amazing. The immediate feedback to the workshop was great. In fact, I even tracked these leaders over the next six months and what was really remarkable were the business results achieved by these leaders. Each leader had reported an increase in business. This increase was in an industry struggling with growth at that time. One of the leaders actually multiplied the top line revenue by three times! Before, the dealership he was leading sold 100 cars. Now they were selling 300 cars. His performance was recognized and rewarded by the company.

It was humbling to note when the leaders said that their journey to this success had started in that February workshop, in the wintry, February night of Delhi, around that bonfire. A workshop run, not by an "industry guru", but by an involved "facilitator".

Vasudha Lal

Vasudha Lal is a Distinguished Toastmaster, educator, inspirational speaker, storyteller and Communication Skills expert. She is a certified Trainer of NLP, Transactional Analyst, practitioner of Nonviolent Communication, coach, mentor and facilitative trainer. She is an active listener and people fondly call her a 'soundboard' and their 'go-to person'. Affable and approachable, she brings her lessons from life with a blend of empathy and compassion.

Whose Game is it Anyway!

Vasudha Lal

The dice rolled on the table and stopped at 3, then at 5 and then at 4 but neither at 1 nor 6. I, like any other player, had three chances to open my account but failed at it. Not my day, I thought to myself. The dice won't comply. Was there a way I could guide it, manipulate it or tell it what to do? Well, no.

Life's dice rolled and gave me 3, 5 and 4 and no more. What started as a corporate career rolled to a wifey's tale and moved me like a dice that wouldn't listen from one roll to another. A couple of months into a realm that I had never tasted, intrigued me to delve deeper. Finding myself in a new environment with people of different seniority and different ranks, different socio-economic strata and different tastes, different cultural backgrounds and different approaches, I lost myself. All of my twenty-five years of early life I had never tasted diversity at such an extreme level. I was baffled at the sheer diversity! My plate was full of cuisines from across the dimensions of the 'Oh so vast country' but my dimensions were limited to how much I wanted to see.

Some were written off by their appearance while some by how they spoke, some, how they conducted, and some wrote me off. A fresh MBA with three years in a corporate house showed me as a stiff upper lip with nose in the air. All else appeared small to my overrated ego.

This was not to last! A quick welcome chat at the chief's house brought my ego to the ground. A man of high authority with humility beyond compare and a wife who matched him in talent and great human care. It was a 45-minute gateway to a life changing experience. Let me tell you, I had married an Army Officer then and that meant a change of life, perspective and dimensional shift from glamour to glory in the truest sense. My attitude, that I was an officer's better half and that too an aviator, glamourized by the outside world; men in overalls and aviators, I was flying high on cloud nine with no wings of my own.

That one meeting over a cup of tea, however, made a paradigm shift and brought me gliding back on mother earth. Thus started another tale of 27 years and is still going strong.

In those 45 minutes, I learned life lessons that have stood by me:

- Lead where required, sometime from behind and sometime from the front.
- Ask and not tell
- Dialogue not debate
- Empower and enable, lest you disable what is innate in all
- Clarity on the role and the role belongs
- Do not let people keep coming back like beggars for a morsel; instead, give them the power while you steer the ship
- Teach them to fish; while you run to count the currency

Thus began my journey into the world of facilitation. Twenty-seven years later, I have ended up asking many questions tailored by design that opened many vistas than answering many queries crafted by design.

Let me let you into how I progressed.

As a battery commander's wife, I had the responsibility of looking after the welfare of 100 families, their well-being and also looking into their familial matters if and when they arose. With a battery of uniformed men and their halves, I would move with a mini entourage but no air. Talking to people about their matters, looking for resolution wasn't easy where resources are scarce and to top it all, no one from the families to hold one's hands. On my first official visit as 'Memsahab', I chose to gather all of them in a common hall and invited them to tea and some snacks. Knowing the diversity in the room and bringing them all to the same page was no mean task. I started with telling them my name and where I came from, what my feelings were, and how I felt in their company. I noticed a sudden shift in their perception of me and they eased in how they sat. I was relieved. I then asked them to play a small game before we moved ahead. I asked the first lady to name herself and look at the one next to her and smile. The second one would name the first one then name herself, turn to the next and pass the baton. At the end of this round everybody knew each other and had begun to accept each other's diversity.

My lesson: Facilitate to Enervate

After giving 20 years to AWWA, the Army Wives Welfare Association in different capacities, I learnt it is optimum to serve with the awareness that every human being has the capacity to think and produce results that they desire. Collective desire needs a process that entails bringing together all the stakeholders, hearing them out and collating what is best for the greater good.

Once it so happened that we had to welcome the better half of the Chief of the Army and that meant GOD of Army. Everybody right from the top bosses to the last soldier was to come up with a plan par excellence. It meant not just to impress but to express solidarity at the station level, bringing all the leaders to agree to a common frame and organise something so magnificent that security remains unhindered and everybody enjoys it too.

With orders coming for everything to be done like this and like that, things had begun to fall apart before the structure even came up. It was time to facilitate a dialogue, my lesson at work! Soon volunteers were asked and groups made with different tasks to tend. People were now animatedly working together and soon a draft was on the table. A little tweaking and stakeholders were ready to play their part with greater care and commitment.

My Lesson: Ask what you have and what you can; Divide and rule to win the game

Life moved on and I got into teaching with no qualification to match. People often say, 'Oh, if you can't do anything, you surely can become a teacher'. Thirty years on, I beg to differ. In a country where teaching is for the sidekicks, the results say it all. You fail in your career, life or relations, don't worry, you can become a teacher. As if the basic qualification for becoming a teacher meant to be a failure first. I scoffed at the thought of becoming a teacher myself while I was playing the role of a management trainee, earning a good sum. I too looked down upon the 'job' of a teacher as down-market.

But soon my perception had changed. I had begun to believe, if you cannot be a teacher, you are worth no job. However, the biggest battle-ground lies in the classrooms at any level, from kindergarten to the IITs, IIMs and corporate boardrooms. The first lessons in leadership begin there.

I was coerced into teaching by the principal of my first child's first school. Her EQ (educational qualification) for me was my Communication Skills and how I engaged people, including children in conversations, with ease. I didn't realise it then that my first lesson learnt over a cuppa tea was still going strong. I felt qualified to teach the tiny tots at the first go; my first vocation after a hiatus. I soon found myself enjoying every single day at work and in fact looked forward to Mondays more than Fridays. Life's meaning had changed for me for good. The adage, 'child is the father of man' was teaching me lessons in leadership and life.

As we moved stations, mapping the nation, I was graduating up the level too. From being a kindergarten teacher teaching A, B, C to becoming a senior teacher, coordinator, officiating Vice-principal, mentor, trainer, coach and editor of school magazine, advisor to the panelists, anchor, script-writer, I had donned all these hats with aplomb. I was conducting FDPs (Faculty Development Programmes), hosting conversations with young adults, bringing difficult conversations to pliable moulds by the aid of that one life changing lesson: ASK NOT TELL.

In 2012, we had to yet again move to another city and another school with 4500 students and 200-odd staff. It was scary. I took my chance and went to speak with the principal. The office had the head of the Department of English sitting there. We got talking and the principal asked for my views on the school environment and how students should be engaged in and out of the classrooms for better results, etc.

In full honesty, I brought to the table my view of the world that had evolved with the experiences of collective wisdom for collective growth over the years. With no EQ to match the post, I was asked to join as a senior English teacher from the very next day; no panel interview nor demonstration class. Nothing at all! There has been no looking back since then. I spent six long years with that institution, donning different hats and have grown in strength from there on. Everybody. including my colleagues and students from all levels would come up to me and say, there is a way with you, how you encourage and inspire everyone to bring out their best. Even a lame could begin to run with you! I would bow and smile to my higher grace. Soon, everyone was pushing me to grow from the precincts of the school curriculum to the bigger canvas of life. They said, 'You are a life-coach for us. Don't stop here.' They wanted me to take my learnings to the wider audience. I felt inspired and nervous at the same time. I had not gone into formal learning mould in a long-long time.

I connected with my friends in Mumbai and enquired about NLP programmes. The ground was set and I flew into Mumbai in August 2013 for my first tryst with life beyond cantonments and academia. I had my first date with NLP and it got me intrigued and I went ahead to become a Trainer of NLP. I was reading more and more about harvesting group wisdom, leading people and understanding hierarchy in organisations. My second and subsequent visits to Mumbai lead me to meet an outbound facilitator who was known to the world of trainers as 'Elephant Ears', someone who hears people patiently, doesn't do anything and harvests results. This had my attention for sure. Bagged and armed to the tee, I made yet another visit to Mumbai. The first ever Train The Trainer (TTF) batch was launched by the same Elephant Ears. The room was full of who's who from the trainers' world, flying in from all over the country. I was intimidated like a tiny mouse caught in a snare!

From day one to the last day I was lost with not a clue as to what was going on in the room. Colour papers flying in all shapes and sizes, chart papers unrolling on the floor, people shifting and sifting in different groups each time the game plan changed. I had no team, yet I was in them all. At the end of the exercises and drills we were made to do, we had walls covered with a sticky blue bed sheet that they called the 'sticky wall'. Each sticky wall had some story to tell that came about in bite-sized papers with scribbles on them. Different shapes: some arrows, some hearts, some triangles and some bubbles apart. It took me back to my kindergarten years. Such craziness with which all of us were deeply engrossed. Sitting on the floor, bending on the tables, popping candies and deliberating hard. I wondered at the sheer energy in the room. And all this while our Elephant Ears with his comrade Tall Man, doing nothing except ringing a tinkerbell once in a while. At the end of the day, they used jargons like divergence, convergence, harvesting group wisdom, ways of working, and what all. I felt like a babe lost in the woods. I was envying the duo, every bit. Do nothing, ask a few questions, let the cats out of the bag, stir the porridge once in a bit and voila you have an amazing outcome, one that they want. I wanted to be that one!

I went back home with a bag full of tools to trade. Soon an opportunity to run a training programme for the faculty came and I set about designing it with questions such as:

- What is the purpose of this training?
- What is the desired outcome the administration wants?
- How many people would attend?
- How much time is allotted?
- What is the space earmarked?

Once armed with clarity, I set about crafting the programme. When I got stuck, I called the Elephant Ears, who now was approachable without fear (my own creation) and shared my concern. He simply heard me out and asked me to put forth four questions in a quadrant and display them on the screen. Break the attendees into groups and work them around these questions. It was that simple, was it? With full faith in my mentor and trust in my new learnings I conducted the sessions. I believed that whatever emerges is what the group wants. Eventually, the outcome was mind boggling. The walls were decorated with coloured bits of papers and sticky-wall. Like fervent ants on a mission the huge auditorium was abuzz with teachers who were now busying DOING and not TELLING. The tables had turned. At the end of our programme, every single attendee came up and thanked me. Their feedback:

- Wish we have more of such sessions. We feel belonged and don't feel disengaged.

- Please take all our trainings hereafter. You not only motivated us but remained in the background.

- Never for a moment did we feel that you were telling us to do instead we felt driven by our own energy.

- We feel justified and heard.

- We are happy with the results; they are ours.

My lesson: Do what you are doing, and before that, know what you are doing and then do that.

A couple of months later I had started to miss what I had learned at Mumbai and wanted to be part of that full-on but wasn't getting a break. Academics does not give full freedom to explore, being bound by a curriculum. And then came a call that gave me an opportunity to work with a well-known facilitator who was looking for a buddy to run a programme at Jaipur. I jumped to the opportunity and travelled to the city in anticipation and excited nervousness. A celebrity facilitator and I, a newbie. We spent two days with a young enterprising team looking for breaking grounds in the corporate world. I was mesmerised by the ease with which the sessions ran. A few ground rules set by the participants, the flow of the session designed to deliver, timelines set, breaks after every 90 minutes, everything was detailed to deliver with precision. The attendees came up with their concerns, their hidden fears, how they could overcome them and what is the way forward to achieve their dreams. All of it through the potent process of divergence, convergence and group harvesting. The highest rule was, 'Let them run their show'. It was yet another feather in my cap, of course with a different colour. I was flying over the clouds for I had tasted life at yet another level.

My lesson: Ask what they know, then ask what they don't know they know and they will know everything they need to know.

By now, I had found my path, my true calling. I now knew what I had been doing for twenty-five long years was exactly that but did not have a name and a known methodology to that. I called it the game of life. And now the game of life had nuances and a laboratory of methods to name. I had found my path.

We finally moved bags and baggage to Pune, a hub of corporate culture that embraced diversity like no other city. I was every bit at home in this city owing to its diversity and inclusivity. My first step was to join a Toastmasters Club here, to build and explore my communication skills and a network to find work and establish myself outside the confines of the defence environment. My first speech fell flat as I was told in a feedback sandwich (a method used for constructive criticism) that I did not understand the purpose statement of my first delivery.

My lesson: unlearn, learn and relearn to establish and earn.

Four months into the city and I was ready to rock n' roll. An opportunity came my way to be part of this amazing world of facilitators, the IAF, International Association of Facilitators. I found myself meeting a gentleman who spearheaded the hub here. Was I scared? Yes, every bit of it! A few minutes into the meeting and the myth was broken. I was inducted into the family of facilitators and thus began the ultimate journey. Every month saw a 3-Dimensional laboratory explore the 3 Ds: design, deliver and develop or meet over a kata conversation to build strong relationships that bonded well and strong or else be part of a learning session facilitated by a member. It has been a journey of sorts.

I have had the opportunity of attending two amazing conferences at the India level. One at Lonavala, hosted by IAF Pune, of which I was a part of the host team and the other at Delhi. I saw coming together of leaders in their own rights, a confluence; 'to give with gratitude'. There were no airs of authority, no keeping away what they have. The mantra that ran in the plenary was, giving with gratitude grows in multitude. It was a mix of seasoned leaders at the international level rubbing shoulders with young managers and trainers, raring to get their attention. What stood apart for me were names like Unhurried Conversations, Wicked Problems, Design Engineering without any Designs to recall a few. Evenings saw up by the campfire though not literally all the time, singing songs and exchanging ideas how not to tell all the time and more importantly asking the right questions. Supreme of all the questions was to ask the right questions and how, was my biggest question that day.

The second conference at Delhi saw us worried about the polluted air of wintry November. A lesser footfall owing to the pollution scare still saw a successful culmination of the first ever landmark event hosted by the IAF Delhi team. I was fortunate to buddy two giants in the industry. The ease with which they conducted their ninety-minutes session opened my eyes wider still. The title was somewhat around the theme of letting go of methods. Somewhere these methods too have become crutches for the facilitative-trainers. It was time to reframe the learnings:

- Can we work without any plan?
- Is it imperative to have paraphernalia?
- What if there is no design?
- Can we design on the go?
- What is paramount to a facilitator?

My mind was reeling with excitement.

My learning: Is the sky only as much as our eyes can see or can we increase our vision by seeing from others' eyes too?

I have moved on in the school of life. I have now become an established speaker, a Distinguished Toastmaster, the highest accomplishment at Toastmasters International. The two institutions par excellence have taught me some profound lessons in life:

- Do not serve what you think you have and you can.
- Ask what their hunger is, prepare with the same ingredients to serve their needs rather than feed what you think you can.
- Respect the need you are serving and let that be your calling.

One thing that stays with me every single day: be the being than being the doer for others' deeds.

It is easy to hold a finger and walk the person across, it is bliss to be the path and watch them walk…

In the Light of a Day

Vasudha Lal

Oh, what does it take to break ice, unmould mind-sets and change road maps? Deep in reflection, thoughts kept flowing, wondering where it all began: from being a do-er to being a be-er.

It was that time of the year when all the facilitators come forward to extend their gratitude to the community of employers et al. It was Facweek 2019, a week in the month of October, celebrated across the globe. I got in touch with the Learning & Development (L&D) Head of a financial giant and proposed a pro bono session during the Facweek. A few emails were exchanged, and they came up with a proposal in place. They had never experienced facilitation so far and were open to taste the savoury 'offered for free'. I had a quick call with the Head to understand the need and outcome from their end; they wanted a two-hour session on:

- **Topic:** 'Engaging Employees Mind and Hearts at Work

- **Attendees:** 25 senior leaders (Regional Heads and above)

- **Objective of selecting the topic:** There has been a lot of chaos in the Non-Banking Financial Company (NBFC) space, and everyone is worried on what and how the future course of business is going to be. Leaders should therefore be in a position to gain confidence of their employees/teams and guide them towards building a positive ecosystem, thereby enabling them to think beyond current volatility and constraints yet commit and deliver their best as usual.

- **Outcomes from the session:** Leaders to be able to gain practical insights on motivating and direct employees/teams towards a cohesive and confident work environment.

All of this sounded exciting. I ran through my repository of PPTs, video clips and training material. And I felt I could simply go and give a motivational talk, play a couple of games to recharge the participants. I could come back home leaving behind a WOW factor in the room. That's it!

The facilitator in me, however, asked me to hold on. I sat rummaging through the data I had and nothing seemed to appeal. I decided to visit the IAF website and check the data available in 'Sessions Lab'. There's a repository of 1200 plus processes that I could choose from, based on the need of the session at hand. I browsed through the eight sub-categories: team, energizer, idea generation, issue resolution, issue analysis, action and skills.

Looking at the needs of the organization, I went about creating a draft. The most exciting part of any session plan for me lies in selecting the icebreaker or the energizer. It is the first knock on the ground that sets the mood. And then comes the bottle neck. Which one to choose and the best one at that. I let the matter be till I was to meet three amazing facilitators who ace their skills. The venue of our meeting was a corporate office where we'd gathered to deliberate on a scheduled session and present among us was someone who brought IAF to India. One of the founding members and a master blaster, a storyteller, an improvisation expert, a dramatist, a master juggler of resources available at hand; someone I have always looked up to. We deliberated upon a lot of things, shared ideas on how the community is growing and how facilitation is the new buzzword in the L&D world. We were two hours into the discussion when I shared my desire to have their view on the upcoming session. They asked me for my plan and I had none. I told them of the session plan and desired outcome. We started discussing one flow after another, but nothing seemed to appease me. I wanted something powerful. Master blaster facilitator came up with a suggestion and I grabbed it right away. I thanked each one profusely and with 3 masala chais down I was ready to rock. I was a week away from the appointed date.

I was getting ready to travel to Mumbai for an engagement with a financial organisation. A backpack and an overnighter in tow, I was set to go. I took out my checklist to verify if I had missed out on any key thing. A night suit, a formal dress for work, shoes, toiletries, and above all my paraphernalia called the facilitator's toolkit. All in place with flipcharts, colour papers, chisel markers, cut outs in different shapes and similar sizes and above all, the sticky wall. I was all set.

I left home early to catch the Volvo buses plying between Pune and Mumbai. Watching the sun amidst the plateaus and hills of Lonavala, I was enjoying every screenshot from the window of the air-conditioned bus and its sealed windows provided. I hadn't had a more exciting trip in a long time. The flow of the session kept playing in my head like an old love song. I spent the night at my friend's place and the next morning, ahead of time, I was already speeding on comparatively clean Mumbai roads scant of daily traffic. Guess I was a tad too early.

I reached the ground floor of the office complex and heard people talking in numbers and money. Well, welcome to the NBFC space! I had a big bag on my shoulder like kids going to school or some dreamy artist with colours and canvas in tow. I was ushered in a swanky conference hall and half my enthusiasm was deflated. I had planned for free space and here I had upholstered chairs to hold my space. One smart room, with waiters moving around serving sumptuous breakfast with steaming coffee. My mind went into overdrive planning my next move. At IAF I had learnt never to fall in love with the processes. Instead, to play with the flexibility of what is opportune in the moment. I saw that I was the only lady in the room full of towering gentlemen. That did not deter me either and I decided to play my Communication Skills to the best.

We soon had leaders of different verticals engaging in an ice breaker activity and getting to know each other well. By the end of the initial 15 minutes everyone knew everyone, and the room was abuzz with conversation. My next step entailed asking a few questions on their unique leadership style. I could see different versions of leadership visible to all. Right from democratic to assertive to intuitive to what have you! Next on the agenda was to have a structure in place and follow it through. WoWs (ways of working) were set. We soon divided the larger group into four teams and asked them to map enablers and derailers of their current challenging situation. Every group deliberated and argued and came up with their own exhaustive lists. Blaming the government of the current policies, economy and the endless list of complaints came pouring forth. I sneaked in some thoughts to ponder with a' how about things that are within our reach and not what we cannot control.' Hmmm, then we will have to restructure the entire process. Animated discussions ensued and out came a list of do-able and some beyond control.

I then asked all the groups to post their findings on the sticky wall and we took a gallery walk to experience all the information available for all. Similarities were apparent in the way groups had collated their thoughts. It was time for the next step. I asked them to map the two extremes and plot a way forward in the middle space deliberately kept free till now.

The groups were asked to come forward one by one as teams and map their ideas on the main wall. Top key pointers were given a score each. In the end all the teams huddled together to see the collective outcome. The key surprise element was the common thought rampant among all teams. This came out as a surprise because no one team knew what the other was doing. A final call to bring out the top five key pointers and deep discussions started. Now everyone wanted to have a say. By now we were nearly 90 minutes into the session.

The final step was to collate all the key elements and pick top five enablers or Forces for Change and five derailers or Forces against Change. Finally, it was time to map them across the delivered 'Change Proposal' by one and all.

There was silence after a while. It was time to call it a day. One feedback that came out loud and clear was, "you made us do everything and you yourself stayed in the shadows, but it was fun deliberating on our own problems, we rarely address."

The cause and the agent drive the process and delivers the outcome, whatever that may be. In the end the stakeholders get what they feed and finally harvest. The facilitator enables a dialogue, asks a few conscious questions and moves to the fringes. I wound up my day that day with a beaming smile and a sense of satisfaction. They kept telling me, "Madam, you didn't do anything except throwing questions at us. This type of training we have never tasted before."

That my friend, is the power of facilitation! It was time to move on.

Parineeta Mehra

Parineeta Mehra is Leadership Communication & Life Transitions Coach, Facilitator, Mentor and Certified Speaker. A professional with over 26 years of experience, she inspires leaders to build awareness and impact they have on others. She helps them create the results they want along with building lasting business relationships. She has worked with executives across the education, financial, health, retail, and technology industries. Her carefree and agile disposition helps her clients feel courage, clarity and confidence in what she delivers.

The Learning Curve to Facilitation

Parineeta Mehra

*"All the world's a stage, and all the men and women **merely** players. They have their exits and their entrances."*

– William Shakespeare

The journey begins: I think I know

As I sit in reflection, I see life as a journey. A stage where we play different roles as Trainer, Coach, Facilitator, and more in our Professional lives. I started my career in sales with space selling in 1990, then moved into event sales and later into insurance sales. Now, in 2020, I sell my coaching and consulting services to individuals and organisations. My aim is to bring in value addition in managing challenging situations, sales funnels, covering employee engagement journey and lots more in that line of offerings. So how did I transition into OD & HR services?

I joined ICICI Prudential in 2002 as an advisor – Sales again. I did well as I got some good results by selling policies to my contacts and their connections. I went on to become an MDRT (an international recognition where you get to go abroad and be with other successful advisors). Life seemed better now but I was feeling something was missing – like the salt in food. Sweet, I had tasted plenty by now, and so it was a given. But let us move ahead by a few years for more perspective on how I landed up in Training and Development.

It all began with ICICI Prudential, when I met Shiv Khera, who is a well-known motivational speaker. I remember I didn't want to stop shaking his hand then, as I felt delighted to have met him. I was what they called a 'Tiger Trainer' in the Tied agency vertical of ICICI Prulife. One could fast track the journey to become a trainer from an independent sales agent, if we met certain sales criteria defined by the system. And that was easy for me to accomplish. As a trainer, I had to do some sales too, so that the advisors could see how conversion happens. We had to 'walk the talk' by showing them how to meet targets by pitching existing/new products, updating agents and managers in the system and so on. We had to also do a communication or motivation session to get individuals to meet desired targets of the system. And all this gave me a great kick as I was good at what I did.

Back then, showing films like 'Miracle Man' or 'Lagaan' in a session on motivation seemed like a badge on my chest that I should be proud of. What did you learn from the film? These characters had difficulties in their lives and they overcame them. They followed SMART goals to get where they wanted. What stops you from getting where you want? As I repeatedly did the sessions week after week, and as they say, anything you do regularly, you get better at it, I got better. Colleagues, clients would call for doubts on products, personal challenges, and that made me feel very important. Actually, it was my ego being pampered by all that typical 'shot in the arm' sessions I was doing back then. I thought I had arrived as Trainer.

Soon, I got an offer from NIS Sparta in 2005 to join in as their Centre manager to drive the L&D Insurance piece there. It was a big move so I accepted and learnt more about how to do the same topic differently. I learnt more on processes like Spanco for overcoming Sales Objection and doing a variety of other Sales and Influencing Programs. This was like in those days moving from a Maruti Wagon Suzuki to a WagonR or a Honda basic series. The gears were different, and I was enjoying both the ride as well as the company of 'learned souls' around. NIS Sparta was a good learning ground where I learnt more about other programmes that I could deliver in addition to the regular ones in the BFSI/Retail sector.

Life Unfolds: I learn, I don't know

One day, a trainer fell sick and wasn't able to make it for a program. I was asked if I would want to take a shot at it because while the client was from the Automobile Sector, I had prior experience of delivering on sales closing programs. I agreed. My profile was shared with the Client and once passed, I was given a briefing on the call on how to run the session two days later. I was all pumped up and went ahead with an intent to capture the client and come back victorious.

Alas, the program bombed! We say bombed meaning it was a disaster, as I couldn't remember all the slides and then got nervous too. I thought I had prepared well enough. I came back home with not only a flat tyre but also a flattened morale and self-doubt. "C'mon, Pari. You've got to pull your socks up. You are a Rockstar" is what I told myself and entered the office the next day. Half a dozen eyes peered in my direction and I felt, oh lord, please help me through this day. Soon enough, I was sitting for lunch as usual with the gang. I recall Rishi, my friend saying, *"Hota hain,* Mehra*ji"*(as he fondly called me back in those days). Ranjit too smiled and reassured me that it's ok, no big deal. The lord had heard my prayers.

I soon forgot the incident and then after a month or two, we had a similar situation. The trainer called last minute to say she could not make it for the program the next day. Phone calls followed back and forth with the client and once again, I became the back-up delivery trainer! I felt like the stepney of the car. Once again, I was booted on the program, and this time by someone senior in the system. I ran the session almost verbatim to them (as a replay) and was ready to hit the floor the next day. This was a time to see how I would land when the rubber meets the road. Once again, I almost failed—it didn't bomb, but the happy sheet scores were not happy when I looked at them. I had been able to draw out participants of different learning styles to some extent but there was more ground to cover ahead.

What followed, is session after session, some pulling through with flying colours, others not so well. I began to feel not only butterflies but also elephants in my stomach now. One day, I went up to my boss and asked, "Do you think I should quit?" "No!" was his reply. He came with a background of sales from Xerox, which was back then, and even today, a known and reputed company. He sat me down and counselled me on how failures are life's best stepping stones. I must confess, I did not fully agree with him back then. When you are young and in your early 30's, you want to win more often and losing seems like the end of the road. It did to me too. I worked there for another year or so, then decided to move on.

Life happens: I get to know

I have always been a risk taker in my career. I believe, you don't take risks. You execute the possibility to see if you get the result you expected! New opportunities, new sessions, new topics, new challenges, and new learnings. It was 2009 and I was a more humbled person now, having conducted nearly 850 sessions – succeeded as well as failed. I learn about facilitative training as a concept and practice some strokes on different canvases and mediums. I am also a proud owner of a semi-automatic vehicle and enjoying my test drives on the highway now. I am learning facilitative training with it nuances and understanding what is different. I have learnt how Facilitative training seeks to help learners construct meaning and come to an understanding of important ideas and processes. Their role in this process is to guide inquiries into complex problems, texts, cases, projects, or situations. I have moved to fine tune and practice gears more effortlessly into a space of unconscious competence. Which means that I have enough experience with the skill that I can perform it almost unconsciously.

In 2010, I was head of Channel Skills Development in a Banking Technology Firm. As head of Field Sales & Training, I needed to manage difficult conversations with the Operations Head and related Senior Heads of verticals. The conversations were sometimes difficult. I learnt to manage the pressure from the business that insisted on conducting training with minimum time, money, and other resources. It has been a tough exercise making them realise that learning takes time and a cycle to follow, for results to show up. I realised I almost gave up after trying to convince the Business heads and the COO. Then, one day when we were in a regular update meeting, I requested them to allow me to guide them to list down and identify by voicing what change they wanted to see and how it would be measured. That actually worked when instead of telling, we were jointly exploring how it is possible.

From then on it was a smoother ride when it came to approval of L&D budget or to an agreement on a roll out of programs on the ground and in regional offices. Over the next two years, I used facilitation wherever I got a chance at work, even though I didn't know it as facilitation in its truest sense back then. My role was to get the Leadership team to recognize the efforts and support training for the services they offered. The challenge was to make them agree to fund the programs. Once we connected with the end audience through the channel partners with processes in place, the ease of work began to slowly fall in place. Investment of time and resources for learning and supporting the right practices for roll out was the uphill task but I overcame it finally.

Life changes: I now know where I stand

It was September of 2014. The sky was clear blue and I was returning from my session on Decoding Communication & Influencing for a senior Leadership Team. Nestled in my seat 6A – window seat – I looked out and saw the clear sky and smiled to myself as I replayed the session in my mind. I had run a session for a large and well-known client. They worked with the United Nations & WHO and were the amongst the biggest in the Social Sector in Asia. The Client business depended on Communication through which they influenced Key sponsors and Govt bodies, etc. The leadership had heard about my training and engagement skills and wanted to see if it would help them instead of a regular route they adopted of presentations. They wanted me to get the leaders to express themselves with more ease and empathy and handle ambiguity without getting stressed. Support the younger lot to navigate change better and express the anxieties they faced. I began the session by using picture cards to help participants share more about themselves to each other. We used the Value Spectrum to understand the knowledge level of Participants on the Subject. This was followed by using the Johari Window with aim of crafting more effective messages by imagining how the recipient will take what you say. I used what I now understand as Conversation Café and Improv to get them to share and then come up with their own solutions that were put up as 'options for way ahead'. They had to then select collectively the top 3 that they chose to follow, for which we used Affinity charts. In such complex discussions where people have different views and interests, good facilitation skills can make the difference between success and failure of the session.

I was still not doing facilitation the way I understand it today. I clearly remember I was getting ready for a session on Leadership styles and Teamwork and as I was talking to a friend whom I happened to chance upon through some connection, he said you know what, you are discussing what process we can do, what else I can do because he called himself a facilitative Trainer. He asked if I would come and attend this event at Taj Vivanta. That was August 2015.

As a facilitator, that was the first National Conference I attended on Facilitation. Later on, that changed not only the way I looked at my delivery, but also my understanding of how Facilitation is delivered.

The definition of 'facilitate' is to make easy or ease a process. The role of a facilitator is to plan, guide and manage a group event to ensure that the group's objectives are met effectively. S/he uses clear thinking, good participation and buy-in from everyone who is involved in the process, right from conceptualisation to roll out of the Intervention. To facilitate effectively, you must adopt an objective mindset. It simply means that, for the purposes of this group process, you will take a neutral stance. You step back from the detailed content and from your own personal views and focus purely on the group process. With the faith that the process will lead the group to their destination. In Facilitation (process of making the group come out with possible solutions by being guided, instead of being shown or told exactly what to do), you will need to use a wide range of skills and tools. Explore what fits post conversations with the Stakeholders. See what fits: is it problem solving, decision making, team management and communications – when the topic is Communication & Influencing? It is critical to have stakeholder conversations before contracting. Only focussing on the facilitation process is not enough. And we need to get them involved so they take ownership of the outcomes.

As I reflected on what I could have done better, I heard an announcement made and that brought me back to the flight. I sat there observing how the crew facilitated conversations amongst the passengers to make them comfortable and have a memorable experience of the flight. I did the same for my client by creating a memorable experience so that they call me again for running their next intervention.

You must have heard the famous TS Eliot lines, that only those who risk going to fail can possibly find out how far it is possible to go. This was the driver of my career and I explored new horizons through new roles that I took up every few years. At heart, I am an adventurous person who loves to explore everything. So I took the risk and got the support to do so, which made me move towards helping people move ahead. The joy I get from that is immense. There was this desire to do something different constantly, and my thoughts changed as life passed and soon enough I was an author of my own life.

What a facilitator does is plan, guide and manage a group event to ensure that the group's objectives are met effectively, with clear thinking, good participation and buy-in from everyone who is involved in the process from conceptualisation to roll out of the Intervention. To facilitate effectively, you must adopt an objective mindset. It simply means that, for the purposes of this group process, you will take a neutral stance. You step back from the detailed content and from your own personal views and focus purely on the group process. With the faith that the process will lead the group to their destination.

I Progress: I now know what I need to know

Ever since I got glued on to facilitation there has been no looking back. The likes of International names like Tom Swartz and Larry Philbrook have helped me gain a better understanding of what this landscape is all about. Doing things differently makes people understand a concept with more ease and better effectiveness. What is needed is certain processes whereby the group figures out the answers to a concern/situation so as to guide them; and to ensure that they stay on track and make progress. And when they are nearing the end of the track, then being around to support them and find the right direction. There are three key elements to arriving there: *diagnosing the issue/s, designing a solution* and *finally delivering the session.* For me, the simplest way of defining Facilitation is to say, "We play the role of a midwife! We see what the challenge is in giving birth to an idea and then what is needed in the moment to make that happen successfully with the least difficulties along the way."

The same follows in Training too but there, it is a standard one-way delivery with the onus on the trainer for ensuring key takeaways. Whereas, in Facilitation, the responsibility is shared with the group, as the 'group knows best' what they want and what will work. Besides, you know you've done your job well when the client reconnects with you. The respect that I got from people in training was immense and that of love, affection, and gratitude, but I still felt something was missing and I am a person who usually gets tired of doing the same thing. I look for what's Next, yes what Next and that is when Facilitation happened.

Initially, I relied heavily on processes but in the last 3 and a half years, I've largely done facilitation differently. If it's a new topic, of course I have to navigate to the shore knowing that the process will take care of taking us there safely. I have failed too but I have learnt that if we follow the process and it is done correctly then you find that people are able to find their own solutions. I first tried this with a manufacturing company. I just remember how the client found value in the Intervention. Group facilitation requires you to know and do your homework and clear contracting well. I learnt that even though facilitation may seem like an ideal approach most times, it may not be the best always. That experience made me aware that I need to focus on how to foster open participation with respect for client culture, norms and participant diversity. How to manage conflict by recognising conflict and its role within group learning. I learnt these lessons the difficult way by failing first and then succeeding.

I Grow, I accept, I change and now know more

Later on, my clients went on to recommend me to others. Experiences like this made me realise that I know learning is happening on different levels and I don't have to have the answers to everything that the teams need. Me getting my understanding of design processes and different levels of interaction was when I attended the Tyagi event. Many others followed, which left me speechless and in awe of the Art of Facilitation. I didn't straightaway jump into facilitation from training. I went on to coaching and from there into group coaching and then facilitation.

Time went by, and I moved ahead, it was 2018 now. I learnt more and more about myself and the more I learnt about myself, one thing became clear, that for me, I found life to be a canvas that I was dying to paint a different colour and every time with a different shade. Each session was like a different palette, different in knowing that every time something new would emerge that painted my personality, my way of learning & thinking too.

Every journey begins with a single step. After working for 25 years in the corporate world, to go independently and try out something new wasn't easy. Lots of questions crossed my mind. How do I get there? Will I be equally impactful with every new audience? I kept thinking about all this and as I travelled from one city to another, everywhere I went I realised I picked up some learning with every single step. When I reflect back, I realise that I was more a presenter who thought she was adding value to others. It's only now that I realise that I get far more satisfaction from what I am doing here, and I'm even more aware about the value, however small, I bring into people's life.

Facilitation has changed me as a person. It has made me realise that it all starts with being prepared for the session. The more you know about the group, the individual personalities and the dynamics at play, the better you'll be able to plan for a successful session and a positive experience. Start off by asking these questions:

- What will the session space look like? How can I best prepare for this?
- What materials do I need to achieve the meeting goals?

For anything that could arise in the moment, it's a given that sessions go differently than planned, especially virtual sessions with break out rooms or jam boards.

Take stock – check if you have created an inclusive environment for divergent views that will pop up. Consider designing a session with structures and activities that appeal to different types of learners and personality types. It could be as simple as arranging a seating plan that is equal and fair, where everyone is on the same eye level, in a circle and with no one's back to anyone else.

In an effective group session, everyone will walk out aligned – on the same page and speaking the same language. To achieve that, you will need to make sure everyone has a chance to be heard and to hear each other. The best way to do that is to flex your active listening skills and encourage your group to do the same too. Mirroring, paraphrasing and tracking the group helps you leverage the whispers in the group with active listening.

Listening in and observing like a fly on the wall. As a timekeeper, you pay attention to what's going on in the room and allow your group to easily track the time for each task. Whatever method you choose, consider giving people warnings as the time for each activity draws to a close. You can say it out loud or hold up a sign, so you don't need to interrupt the group's workflow or conversation.

There are times where I'm facilitating a session and I care about the content and have an agenda (and a sponsor who has an agenda) as far as what I need from the group. At such times, I know, I'm not content neutral. I'm trying to use the skills of an effective facilitator, knowing that I will weigh in on what the group decides and discusses. I then try to be honest and clear about what role I'm playing (group member or facilitator) to avoid confusion in the audience and set expectations on delivering on desired outcomes in specifically designed ways.

So if you're interested in making things, and creating dramatically better ways of working, then question the process and deep dive into how it serves the purpose you want fulfilled. What colour is your ink? What shade do you practice most? What gear do you ride most? Context and Process are Key – remember that. The rest follows. It is like having a Google Map to follow when lost, but largely relying on gut and your knowledge of the roads that you are driving through. Be mindful about your role in each session – are you a neutral party there to facilitate the process or are you actively invested in the outcome? Then adjust your participation to fit the experience, and you will come out successful.

Facilitation is like a human lab, in that it helps you to figure out a lot more about the human design. In fact, I have learnt a lot about human beings ever since I moved into facilitation and Coaching. I don't think I would have learnt had I continued to be in training, because Training doesn't give you that complete 360° view. It only gives you an overall helicopter view. Does that not suffice to help you drive those results? Yes, but at a very elementary level. If you are looking at bringing in behavioural changes, then one needs to use facilitation along with other methodologies to see higher levels of ROI in the Kirkpatrick Model. It's been a journey on a road with different surfaces. I am grateful that I got to play on these different kinds of roads to experiment where life will take me and how I landed up being a better facilitator, a better human being in the process.

I learnt to facilitate my life and career graph through this process of exploration and lo behold, here stands version X.0 of the person I am. I've just flown a few thousand miles in this sky and only painted a few more shades of grey! There's lots still to learn, as changing times bring in new learnings at each level. A Facilitator in the making – miles to go before I sleep, and I can say I have truly arrived there.

Riding the Wave to New Shores

Parineeta Mehra

In April 2020, the world turned upside down with a 'new normal' that we began to experience and that was here to stay, irrespective of which part of the world we were in. Virtual facilitation and training became more relevant than ever. Not that it was unknown, but only that it was to become a norm in the months to follow. Suddenly, everyone everywhere in the world moved on to virtual engagements. Learning began happening on virtual platforms to ensure that 'support continued unhindered.'

I was invited by a Multinational Organization to run a session on empathy and resilience in the new normal. The need was to show the leadership how to be more empathetic; how to not mix following through on timelines and deliverables with their actions. In addition, the senior team of the Organization needed support to be more accommodative and resilient in handling the younger team members. The younger team had been feeling stressed by multi-fold pressures. As I type this and recall the entire discussion that lasted over 3–4 days, I am feeling the weight of the problem. So I can imagine, how it was for them, back then. I was wondering what to do and how to proceed since I had major internet bandwidth issues. Just then the doorbell rang.

It was an old friend and neighbour, who had lost her parent in these times. She is a senior leader in the Banking Space and was facing similar challenges at her workplace. A few days later, I asked her how she was coping and if she could help me think through the session flow. As she narrated her own experience of 'hanging in there', I found some clues that helped me design the intervention. I thought to myself, looks like the Universe is conspiring to support me and make the session go through seamlessly.

The International Association of Facilitators–India began what they called, 'Wave 1', a series of online sessions to be conducted on Zoom, to engage the community in the midst of the lockdown. This proved to be 'divine timing' and a boon too! Here was my chance to see how ready I was to deliver on the topic. I was amongst the first to take up the responsibility to present a session to my revered audience of experienced facilitators.

I thought, what better opportunity than this to try the topic out. Any art or skill like Facilitation needs practice and if you haven't been doing so, challenges show up. That day, the internet played awry and the rain gods too added to the chaos, apart from the session throwing up multiple challenges. Not once, but many times, the connection dropped for few seconds and then was back again. Phew! The internet had gone awry and my patience was really tried that day like never before in this space! But every time I came back with a greater determination to see the session through. I must say, I was lucky, as the Facilitators supported and stayed calm through it all. A co-fac (short form for Facilitator) was there to help me glide, rather, ride through the wave then. He was there to help me navigate the *Mentimeter* – a tool used to capture responses online, break out rooms in Zoom, and reading out what came up on the chat. The session concluded well. Their feedback was largely positive and supportive. I felt confident. Although, I had not got any leadership team to attend the program, I had my fellow community give me authentic feedback on what needed to be done differently.

The next day, I sat and made a list of items that I call 'penny drops.' They were as follows:

- Know your audience really well. In this case, although I knew them, I had written all my thoughts down (like I normally would for a session).

- Zoom as a platform had been used very sporadically so far. I was not familiar with all its tools.

- Network issues persisted but I still went ahead. I should have made alternate arrangements. Or called in to say, I cannot do it today, which I didn't!

With all this and more running through my head, I collected myself, as I wrote a mail to the client. It said, I am ready to have a discussion on the session to explore what I had in mind. I was now feeling courageous with rediscovered clarity and confidence in what lay ahead. My meeting went well. I landed the assignment! The session on Empathy and Communication in Current Times was delivered and we had a repeat of it as well. The client got back a few weeks later to share that their conversations were beginning differently. The leaders were making a conscious effort to 'keep the young team in mind'. They were asking questions like: How do I show up as a different leader? What kind of role model do I want to be for the younger lot? Where is the struggle? What mindset is being displayed and what is it that I really believe it to be now? They were now willing to let the team to take break/s when they wanted, trying to be considerate when asking for them to stretch beyond regular hours. They began something called 'Waddling Wednesdays'. Every Wednesday (as it's the midweek), the younger lot would narrate their experiences with the senior team over a platform. How they had waddled with small steps to reach where they wanted and were making some progress, however small. The team was now confident that they would make some good progress with future engagements lined up for the next two quarters.

So, what did this teach me or rather help me learn? That facilitation can and does have an Impact. Even if it is facilitating a dialogue and creating space for that to happen. Only, it takes a different kind of preparation on a virtual platform. And there, the biggest lesson learnt was Prepare, Prepare, Prepare! I cannot stress on it enough.

I was left feeling that I had barriers coming in the way of my being ready to deliver virtually that I had to overcome, in order to figure out how I would navigate the sessions with the leadership ahead. Every experience leaves one a tad richer like it left me, and the others who rode that wave with me then. We had learnt what it takes to do facilitation online and how it is so different from the in-person experience. What makes it work and what doesn't – lots of learning got sharpened. I have emerged a butterfly in this space and am now going from flower to flower, picking up and also giving more of what I can. For as they say, there's a lesson to be learnt from everything we do.

Experience is like the fragrance of the flowers from which we get the nectar. It leaves you feeling enriched and empowered to want to ride the next wave ahead. I had used my passion for facilitation to make inroads and build an Impact that got noticed even in the lockdown! I had grown in my engagement style in the virtual space too and that added value to my journey like a feather in the cap. I had ventured into new shores and found my way to wade through successfully.

Nitin Welde

Nitin Welde is a Leadership Coach and Facilitator. He is an Air Force Veteran and recipient of a Gallantry award from the President of India. He has a unique style of correlating his frontline leadership experiences to the corporate environment. He is passionate about Experiential Education, Team Building, Leadership, Oratory skills, and Applied Improvisation. An avid golfer and movie buff, Nitin keeps participants at the centre of all behavioural interventions.

Facilitative Air Warrior

Nitin Welde

Facilitation from the Highest Battlefield

I woke up to the sound of firing and asked my senior, "Is this normal here?" He responded, "Welcome to the Siachen Glacier, my boy. Welcome to the highest battlefield."

I was a young officer when I had come to the glacier. A mere boy of 25, and early on itself I had realised that there would be challenging times. When we woke up, the air was tense and when we slept it was even more so. Every single day was an incredible test of endurance and mental fitness as temperatures ranged from -15° to -30° Celsius. I would step out into a harsh morning air, the wind whipping around me. My eyes would sting quite a bit and it took some time to get used to both the extremely low temperatures and the high altitude. The usual work went on around me, seemingly undisturbed by the weather. The daily routine was tough to keep up with, but we were stubborn to the core. Being a Siachen Pioneer meant one had to look at life differently. The way we took up challenges is encapsulated in our motto:

We do the difficult as a routine
The impossible may take a bit longer

Within the first two days in the glacier, I realised I was about to witness some real challenging times. The altitude of the base camp was 11,600 feet and any usual work there was a challenge in itself. As I landed in my first sortie at the forward post, I was overwhelmed thinking about the challenges of soldiers at the posts. For those who are lucky enough to have never seen a war post, keep it that way. It's a shock, most of the times, keeping pilots and soldiers alike awake at night. Soldiers at an average post would live in cramped up places in extreme temperatures and what was incredibly upsetting, was that these able men could lose lives even in an attempt to keep up with daily sustenance. It is while observing such challenging situations that I realised that I had special interest in human behaviour sciences. While a few of my fellow colleagues were intrigued by the sheer enormity of the tasks at hand, I was also looking for what drives people's behaviour. I was the curious Air Warrior wanting to understand human dynamics more than my other colleagues.

Our unit's main responsibility was as a service provider of things such as ration, kerosene, medicine, etc for the troops at forward posts. My seniors then were an extremely encouraging lot and they used to hand over the responsibility of coordinating with Army units to young officers like me. There were occasions when there were conflicting demands by two or more people, and each had their own interest as paramount. When I observed carefully, I realised that sometimes a different approach than the usual reaped a better output. The telling and controlling approach seemed to prolong the discussions and at end of it all, each were only half satisfied. I started experimenting with more inclusive and more involving dialogue. My approach was to let different groups seek a mutually agreeable solution. As a service provider, we were ready to deliver in the manner and to the extent that was mutually acceptable to all. My senior gave me some wonderful insights into leadership: "Nitin, the requirements will never be equal to resources. That constant struggle will have to be juggled by you. The way you manage the juggle will slowly differentiate you from others." I was immediately hooked on this aspect of leadership. I then saw multiple examples of this being true. I also learnt one important lesson: Whenever possible, social contracting is one of the best ways to find a solution to a group problem. This can be effectively achieved by acknowledging the needs and offers of the group. There is little achieved if you try this with an iron fist. Thus were sown the first seeds of facilitation.

Facilitative Instructor

Soon after the glacier tenure, I was selected to undergo a course in instructional techniques at Flying Instructors School, Chennai. Though the primary purpose of the course was to learn how to be a flying instructor, we were also introduced to the methods of instruction too. As I completed the course, I became aware of the interest that I had developed in the subject of Learning and Development. On completion of the course, we were all ready to teach flying to cadets at the Air Force Academy. Teaching flying is an extremely challenging task. The skills that you have developed have to be transferred to the cadet. The stakes while transferring such skills are very high as one mistake can be dangerous enough with catastrophic consequences. If teaching flying is a challenge, learning how to fly is a double challenge.

In the initial days of learning, an average pilot is always lagging behind the situation. In such early learning phases, it is the spare mental capacity which makes the new pilot capable of assimilating the learning. This essentially means that the learning environment is a typical mix of rote learning as well as experiential learning. The cadet is able to fly due to a mix of skill and self-belief. This self-belief aspect needs greater understanding of behaviour psychology and its effects on our thinking. As I was always intrigued by learning psychology, I started to pay more attention to how I was creating a space for my learner. For me, the learner was able to learn only if I create a good rapport with them. This rapport creation was possible, only If I kept my judgemental behaviour to a bare minimum. The cadet had the liberty to express themselves without having the fear to be themselves. The military establishment has its own share of a hierarchy-based learning environment. In spite of this, I felt that the learner needed to shed off all his inhibitions and be himself. Only then, learning was possible in a real sense. I remember one sortie where I was trying to be too pushy to the cadet, and all up in the air at 10,000 ft. he roared like a lion, "Sir, I don't feel like learning from you, I am scared of you." That day, it hit me like a stone. Indeed, the single responsibility I had was to create a safe space for my learner. I made a conscious effort to ensure that my knowledge and expectations don't suffocate my cadet. As I became more experienced, I devised my own ways to seek transition from a 'Telling Approach' to an 'Asking Approach'. By the end of the term, we were two mature professionals discussing the mistakes. The tenure in the Air Force Academy was extremely gratifying as I experienced the sheer joy of the transition of a raw cadet into a capable pilot.

Team Facilitator

My next instructional tenure was in Bangalore and here I was teaching newly commissioned officers the nuances of flying a multi-crew helicopter. From a 'One on One' learning environment, I found myself interacting with three learners at the same time. The pilot was the fulcrum of this crew, so his understanding of various aspects was extremely important. I was however conscious that each learner was contributing to make it one effective team. This tenure also involved more common understanding as the crew for the helicopter was a mix of people from different cultural, social and educational backgrounds. A more interactive and inclusive learning approach was required due to different learning patterns and experience of learners. I was enjoying my impact on my learners and therefore, I decided to upgrade my instructional qualification to become a Master Instructor. This was a totally voluntary effort and it meant I had to put in 8–9 hours of studies in addition to my routine job. My endurance paid off and I finally upgraded to being a master instructor. When I look back, my inner need to be an effective instructor was so high that I was willing to put in innumerable hours of hard work. My upgradation to master instructor had paid off well as I was selected by the Government of India to lead a training team to Namibia.

Diplomatic Facilitator

One of the most important and enjoyable benefits I had of upgrading my instructional qualification was that I was selected as a Team Leader of an Indian Air Force Training Team to Namibia. My skills as an instructor had to go through a change as per the learner. A learner in Namibia was quite different than a learner in India. There were cultural differences and differences in the way an average Namibian looked at a learning environment. With my Indian experiences of teaching, I thought I had aced the teaching philosophy. But I was in for a surprise, as in the first two months I realised that I had to modify my teaching once again to suit the learner.

The teaching and interaction style had to include more inclusive dialogues. On another front, as a Team Leader this was my first exposure to a leadership role and that too in a foreign environment. I had to represent our team's interest as well as take into consideration the offering by the host country. My interactions with high ranking Namibian government officials made me realise that it was important to make your point in the most assertive yet polite manner. One must also always be mindful of cultural differences and what makes an impact is the respect and understanding that you have of local culture and systems.

My second diplomatic assignment was to Indonesia, where I was to undergo the prestigious Leadership and Command Course. The medium of instruction in this course was Bahasa Indonesia, and this meant I was going to have an extended tenure abroad. I was to learn the language for the first 10 months and then undergo the course for the next 10 months. This was an entirely different experience to interact and learn in a native language.

During the language course, we were 22 officers from 14 different countries, and I was nominated as a representative of all Foreign Officers. This meant that I had to use my people skills in reaching an acceptable solution and that was possible only through more inclusive deliberations. During the main course, I was tasked to moderate discussions on various topics. This is when I became mindful of keeping my opinions, biases and perspectives to a bare minimum. There were officers from many countries and hence diversity and sensitivity towards participants was something I reflected upon after each session. Moreover, all these challenges were to be handled with my command over a newly acquired language.

During one such moderation, I had to keep quiet as I was unsure of my language as well as the impact of my opinions on the group. After the prolonged session, the Senior Staff walked up and said, "Hey Nitin, very well done. At a particular point during the session you just kept neutral by remaining silent. You let the group dive deep to find a solution. Your patient waiting helped them reach a consensus." Little was the staff aware that my silence was an outcome of my inability to express myself in Bahasa Indonesia. That was the day when I understood the power of silence as an impactful tool. The power of remaining neutral in content and in context was clear to me.

On most occasions we were discussing geopolitics and each member had his country's view to project and protect. These discussions were very volatile in the given context and therefore required greater mindfulness in conduct as a moderator/facilitator. I self-reflected on many occasions and understood that opinion-neutral and inclusive conversations have greater impact on group outcomes. This conduct and skill got noticed by the staff at the college and on a few occasions, they invited me to moderate during discussions for a larger number of participants. My hard work and full interest in the learning environment was greatly appreciated by all staff and it bore good fruits. I was happy to make India proud by being adjudged "Best Foreign Officer" of the course.

Guru of Gurus

On repatriation after the Namibian assignment, I was happy to be posted as Staff in Flying Instructors' School with an assignment of 'Train the Trainers'. I had already got 6 years of instructional experience and I looked forward to the new role. Two years in Chennai was a great revelation for me as a trainer. The student officers there were ace pilots who had 7–9 years of flying experience. They had a hands-on experience of operations in the most challenging situations and therefore, they had their past experiences to relate.

In the initial few months, I was struggling with a particular trainee and sought advice from the Chief Instructor. "Sir, I see that in spite of my wanting to give so much, my trainee is unable to grasp my teaching. What could be the problem, sir?" A senior instructor, a man with a prolonged instructional experience responded, "Nitin, your own experience and perspective is making your teaching more restrictive. Just let go of your expertise, and your pupil will discover his own learning. Since the trainee officers come with an abundance of experience, an approach of 'do it because I say so' will not reap good results." Such an awesome piece of advice that I never looked back in my journey of facilitative teaching after that.

I began to really enjoy the facilitative discussions with all my trainees, and it was more of a friendly discussion where at some point we were peers discussing our experiences and correlating with the instructional technique. Like my earlier tenures, I had a clear demarcation between safety aspects and accuracy aspects. The safety aspects were delivered with a 'do it because I say so' approach while the other aspects were discussed more from a facilitative approach. I was extremely happy that I had upgraded my instructional category and because of that I was given the tag of 'Guru of Gurus'. My approach towards a learning environment had undergone a transformation and now it was a 'we learn together' approach rather than a 'I teach, you learn' approach.

Facilitative Leader

I had evolved as an effective facilitator over a period of time. From "I am telling you, just do it" in the year 2001 to "let us discuss, deliberate and evolve together as co-learners" in 2010, I had seen a change in myself. This was the result of the external environment as well as my own internal transformation.

As a Flight Commander of an operational unit, I had to maintain a balance of the telling/asking/facilitating approach. The type of interaction was based on the problem statement and the expected outcome. In more ways than one, I had to use my understanding of behaviour science. This was done in order to reach the most applicable and acceptable solution. It was of extreme importance that we kept moving like one strong team and this was only possible when there was great rapport with each team member. On multiple occasions, I had to just hold the space and listen to people in order to reach consensus. As a good mentor, I realised it was important to ask the correct questions. I began to dwell in the art of questioning and that made personal interactions rewarding. As a senior leader, it was essential for me to remain engaged with my pilots. One of the things that I realised was that we all are a result of our experiences, which has impacted our own upbringing. Each of us have a specific behaviour pattern and it was futile to compare one with another. This meant that I would have to use a customised approach when dealing with each challenge. I realised in this tenure that I enjoyed the group as well as one on one interactions when posed with a behavioural challenge.

The most coveted assignment for any officer from the Armed Forces is Commanding Officer. As a Commanding Officer it was my task to keep the unit in a battle-prepared state all the time. My team consisted of airmen and officers of which 35% of officers were Women Officers. In this role, I realised that my listening abilities, questioning abilities and the ability to build consensus were indeed emerging as my strengths. Being in Delhi area there were enough pressures, however I kept the team motivated by one default setting: "I trust you and you have done your best". This mantra gave enough benefits and was a very satisfying tenure. The hierarchical setting of Armed Forces makes one believe that facilitative leadership is not for the armed forces. I am convinced that like for any other organisation, facilitation can be made a way of group interaction even within the armed forces. It can be very effectively used in various areas and discussions where inclusion and group solution can be fully exploited.

Facilitative Trainer

On handing over Command, I got posted as Directing Staff at the Military Institute of Technology, Pune. Here I was interacting with very senior officers of all three services who were undergoing a year-long Staff and Leadership course. The curriculum involved leadership development and I enjoyed interacting with student officers. Unlike the technical curriculum, any behaviour curriculum has its own challenges. The students are very qualified and experienced and therefore it is important to be an effective facilitator and co-learner. This makes learning an interesting affair for you as well as for the participants.

Like any other mixed group of people, they were always differing solutions to the same challenge. I enjoyed holding my quiet space because then the discussions generated more and more differing perspectives. The solutions may or may not be agreeable to each leaner, however it helps to explore alternatives. A learning environment is, ultimately, an intersection of 'what the teacher wants to drive home' and 'what the student wants to take home'.

I was ready now for my second innings and was keen to understand the Learning & Development in the corporate.

Corporate Facilitator

On seeking premature retirement, I was excited to understand more and more about the Learning & Development in various sectors of society. My interest ranged from giving motivational talks in schools and colleges to conducting training in corporate environments as well. I was fast networking with trainers and new learnings kept me constantly motivated.

A school friend, Shalaka Gundi, introduced me to the International Association of Facilitators in April 2016 and the first session was interesting enough. In the succeeding months, I continued to attend sessions done by the IAF Pune Hub. IAF is a world body that is passionate about spreading the Power of Facilitation. During the sessions, many experienced facilitators presented their thoughts on the concept of facilitation, however I found it to be too overwhelming to be used in its entirety. I had been in a learning environment for the last 15 years and was still not convinced that pure facilitation was so easy to implement. I was extremely sceptical as I thought that there was a certain rigidity in the offering on the table. Then came my Aha! moment when I attended a session by Ajit Kamath, an experienced facilitator. The discussion on that day led to a better understanding of Group Process Facilitation. This diagram said it all:

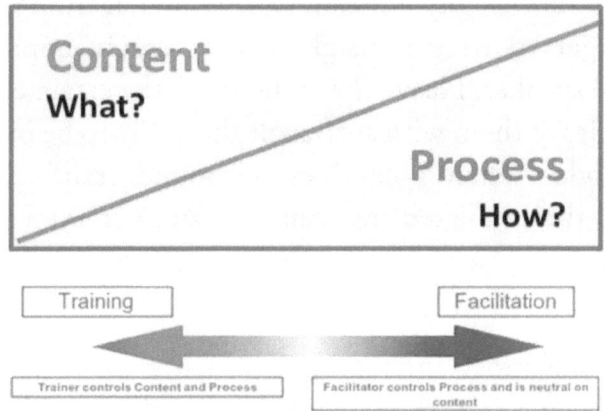

As time passed, I got a better understanding of the concept of facilitation. In my opinion every behavioural intervention, whether at personal or group level can be depicted on the above given diagram. I had the opportunity to present two sessions at IAF's India conference and each of them were well received by the participants. Innumerable discussions on this topic has only reinforced my understanding of various concepts associated with facilitation skills.

In addition to being a proud IAF member, I was also understanding other forms of behaviour intervention. I was fascinated by the medium of Outbound experiential training. During my interaction as a facilitator at High Places Pvt Ltd, I learnt that our insights can be triggered through various simulations in physical dimensions. All responses are 'Here and Now' and this makes it easier for participants to be at their most authentic selves. As an effective facilitator, you can trigger insights by placing a metaphorical connection between simulated and real situations. I found outbound training to be an extremely effective medium of intervention.

I have been doing training, facilitation, motivational talks, coaching, and outbound training for the past four years. I have realised that during any human behavioural learning, the ability of the engager to trigger insights is extremely important. As a motivational speaker, I leave the audience with certain examples and questions. I leave them with sufficient thoughts to be in a reflective, thinking mode. When I conduct outbound training, I am also conscious of the simulated environment, and I create a safe space so that my participants are able to reflect and process their behavioural responses.

One of the most interesting moments on a personal front for me has been a remark by a HR leader who is an influencer on LinkedIn. He had attended my talk, 'Tales of Siachen: Lessons of Leadership'. He was extremely impressed by my delivery and my presence. Two months later, I did a session with the IAF Pune hub and was using Applied Improv as a tool for facilitation. At the end of the session, the gentleman walked up to me and gave me a candid debrief, "Nitin, you are much different today. I did not see the super speaking that you exhibited during your motivational talk."

I responded, "Sir, did you feel engaged during the session? Did you feel we could trigger a few inner thoughts or perspectives? Did you feel that there was any specific agenda or perspective that I was persuasively trying to get across?"

He replied, "No Nitin, it was a very good engaging and insightful session, and it was very impactful too."

I realised that he was expecting me to be 'Speaker' Nitin Welde while I had made a conscious effort to present myself as 'Facilitator Nitin' Welde. This transition was a moment of personal victory.

While my journey has been long and fruitful – and continues to be so – here are three important reflections so far:

- The ability to transform, from a motivational speaker (Sage on Stage) to pure facilitator (Guide on Side) is one of the best abilities I have developed over the last few years. This transformation is not easy at times, however, I am mindful of my own resistance and I feel overjoyed that I am improving on it each day.

- One of the basic tasks in any behavioural intervention is to keep the participants' interest alive. At some level, each Speaker/Facilitator/Trainer/Coach needs to ensure that participants remain engaged. This engagement can be achieved through a variety of methods. From Motivational speaking to Group Process Facilitation, participants can't be disengaged. We need to give sufficient thought to this important aspect.

- In adult learning, we need to have the intersection of past experiences and future transformations. The past experiences come out as sub conscious responses to various simulations/triggers. The future transformation needs more mindful thought. Story Telling, Lego Serious Play, Outbound training, Applied Improv – all these are triggers to make participants seek insights and then plan an effective transformation. While the trigger happens in these sessions, the reflections, and action plan happens after these sessions. We must plan such effective processes and triggers that leave a remarkable impact on all our participants.

As compared to delivering sessions the more important aspect is to be a facilitator and making facilitation a way of life. Each human interaction which is designed to get some outcomes needs to be thought through from the lens of facilitation. The pillar of competencies are so strong that they will deliver the desired results. It needs a small step of self-reflection after each interaction. As we make a conscious efforts to master this wonderful craft, we will surely move from doing facilitative work to being a facilitator.

Facilitation Has Impact

Nitin Welde

Context

The corona pandemic had affected the entire world. India announced its lockdown on 25 March and phase two continued till 3 May 2020. At the end of phase two, the Pune Municipal Corporation gave various relaxations for business and other essential services. However, the municipal commissioner had not clearly stated the policy for re-joining of domestic workers in various housing societies. This decision was left to individual societies without any specific guidelines. On 07 May 2020, the Management Committee of our housing society decided to have an emergency meeting to discuss this contentious issue. I have been a member of this society for the past 5 years and I, in most meetings, actively participate. I am more than happy to articulate my thoughts on issues ranging from security to sanitation. I have volunteered to look into security preparedness of the society and advise the Management Committee on security issues.

Preparation

Our society has three building and the total number of members are 188. The meeting was held at 3PM in the car park of one of our buildings. Around 45 members were seated in a large, circular format due to social distancing norms. As I reached the meeting, the chairman made a special request to me, "Welde sir, please conduct the proceedings today. Things are quite heated up and this may end up in a conflict situation. We need to reach some decisions acceptable to most members, therefore, please make this work."

I had ten minutes to give a thought to what and how I was going to carry out the assigned task. For the past few months, I had been challenging myself to hold a space as a good facilitator. One of the self-given challenges was to not voice my opinions and make it conversations inclusive. I quickly made a plan in my mind conforming to basics as learnt in IAF.

Execution

- Check-in: Once I was handed over the space by the Chairman, I clarified my role as only an Enabler with no specific brief on achieving any given outcome. A quick check-in with the group made everyone aware that all were as anxious and guarded about the impact of COVID and the associated safety measures. There was an instantaneous feeling of 'we are in the same boat'.

- Way of Working: This was suggested, and quick social contracting was ensured to make it binding for all to follow.

- The first issue discussed was whether to allow domestic help to come to the society. Each member was encouraged to express themselves. Clearly, it was emerging that there were two groups: one wanting domestic help and the other not wanting so. All members were encouraged to stay within the boundaries of the question as regards domestic help and not move to other associated discussions.

- Any attempt to take the discussion beyond this scope with 'If… then…' discussions were dealt with a firm yet courteous manner. Unheard voices, senior citizens, and members with patients at home were encouraged to express themselves. The immediate response of one group to another group's opinion was avoided and dealt with a firm yet non-authority manner.

- After all the members had got an adequate opportunity to express their opinions on the question, we summed up the process by voting with a show of hands for ascertaining the mood of the group. With the decision in favour of one group, the other group members were again given a chance to express themselves if they still had a serious suggestion/ objection.

- Having attained the first objective of consensus on allowing domestic help to report to work, we moved towards the guidelines. A scribe was invited and initially we ideated on the precautions to be taken. Free flowing ideas – without judgment passed on its ease/difficulty of implementation – ensured that everyone felt involved in giving ideas to make the entry of maids in the safest possible manner. Once all the ideas were captured by the scribe, we went on to defining the processes for ensuring the entry and exit of domestic help.

- The way forward was also agreed upon and members volunteered to have close liaisons with the Management Committee. It was also agreed upon that in case of any new developments, the management committee could revert this decision.

- A quick closing circle ensured that all members went back satisfied, heard, and most importantly, assured that the personal health of each member would not be compromised at any cost.

Personal Reflections

- I have been a member of the International Association of Facilitators since 2016. I have always believed that group process facilitation is an extremely effective way while interacting with groups. This was one place I got to practice the theory.

- There was hardly any time for me to design the session, which had a time limit of 75–90 minutes. I simply followed the basics as learnt in IAF. A few guiding pillars were: Check-in, WoWs, Guiding the group, Inclusion, Convergence, and Content neutral.

- Throughout the session, I was mindful of different perspectives and my actions were as non-judgmental as possible. I was most mindful of the brief by the Chairman of reaching a consensus on such an important decision.

- I am an Indian Air Force pilot and have had the most amazing experience of operations in action and in peace. I have always enjoyed the spotlight and therefore enjoy delivering motivational talks. I enjoy being the subject matter expert and really love to hold the space, wearing an expert's cap. For past few months, I have been challenging myself to hold the space without being vocal and display an ease in being an *Enabler* rather than an *Influencer*. After the session, I realised that my learning from IAF has been phenomenal. Multiple sessions and interaction with the wonderful IAF community has calmed me down in that aspect and now I enjoy the space as being an enabler to help a group achieve objective.

- This unplanned and impromptu session gave me a sense of satisfaction that IAF and learning from IAF has become my second nature. This transition for me is really satisfying as well as gratifying. The proof of a session well-received is that we had no issues in implementing tough control measures and all stake holders were willing to be involved in making the process better

In my view, there is no better way to experience the power of facilitation.

Sushma Banthia

Sushma Banthia is a Leadership Coach and Facilitator. Sushma has over 40+ years of work experience of which over 20 have been in the area of training and people development. Her passion lies in helping leaders enhance their leadership skills and subsequently enhancing the performance and lives of their subordinates. She believes that this transforms lives not only of the people she comes in contact with but also that of their families and future generations. Sushma loves learning and challenging herself to get out of her comfort zone.

Nirvana through Facilitation

Sushma Banthia

About four years ago, as I was leisurely having my cup of tea one evening, my mobile rang. It was from a dear friend. "Sushma, I have some great news for you. This time the IAF (International Association of Facilitators) conference is in Chennai. You just have to come. I am sure you will find it useful." Her excitement rubbed off on me and I decided to attend the conference. I signed up and became a member of IAF. Implicit trust that my friend would only give me the correct advice.

I had been an independent consultant in the area of training and coaching for over 15 years. Over time, I had learnt the art and science of training, the rough edges had become smooth and I was very comfortable delivering sessions. I had also been conducting online sessions from the comfort of my home for international clients. At the start of my training sessions, I used to introduce myself and tell the participants, "I am a facilitator and the sessions is going to be interactive". The thoughts that ran through my mind: I have already been doing facilitation, what more could there be? New games? New techniques?

Eager and curious to understand facilitation and to learn to how to make my training programs more interesting and impactful, I landed in Chennai. This was to be my formal entry into the world of facilitators. Little did I know at the time, what I was in for!

I arrived at the hotel, in time for the registrations and then entered a huge hall. The warmth with which I was greeted by various people was amazing. They made me feel so welcome. During the conference, I went from one session to another and absorbed all the activities. I noticed that all the sessions had a 'sticky wall' with lots of colourful paper in different shapes/sizes and different props. I was starting to hear certain words/phrases like 'process' and 'content neutral', which made little sense to me. I decided that this must be the language of these facilitators, and by and by I would get to learn it. Drifting through the entire conference from session to session, I was meeting new people and enjoying myself.

The sessions, however, did seem very similar to the type of training session that I was used to conducting. So, what was facilitation? Was I already a facilitator? By the time the conference ended I understood that even though I used to call myself a 'facilitator', what I was doing was 'facilitative training'. There was so much more for me to learn about what facilitation was and wasn't.

While traveling back to Bangalore, I was having a chat with the IAF Bangalore-hub lead. She suggested that we should all run the sessions we attended so that members of the Bangalore hub could benefit, and we could learn from each other as well. Eager to learn, experience and share, I volunteered to run the session conducted on 'Icebreakers and Sociometry', which had been conducted by Ajit Kamath.

Since I was to conduct the session a few weeks after the conference, I started my preparation in earnest and connected with Ajit to get his permission and tips.

Advice from Ajit: Don't try to replicate. Use the concept and make it your own.

It was music to my ears. I was uncomfortable trying to replicate. The situation was different, the audience was different, the number of participants were different, so how could I replicate? Would it make sense?

I reflected on all that I had experienced at the Chennai conference. What new techniques would I like to try? I decided to put up quotes on the wall and get people to identify with one and discuss it within and across groups. I thought of getting them to rate themselves on where they were on a scale of 'training to facilitation'. I learnt that these are **Processes** and are called 'Quotes Connect' and 'Rating Scale' respectively. Keeping a session interactive and asking questions was a skill I already had.

The feedback I received from participants was, "It was awesome" or "Very engaging" or "Learnt a lot". Internally, I felt good as this was my very first session with IAF.

Knowing that I had a lot to learn about facilitation, I started attending the monthly sessions conducted by the Bangalore hub. Every session was engaging as well as a learning experience. The networking was great, I also got to know these wonderful people. What was amazing was how willing they were to share processes, designs and support each other. Most were independent consultants and competitors, and yet, here they were, so willing to help each other. I had never experienced this type of collaboration before.

When it comes to learning though, patience is definitely not my strength. I now wanted to go much deeper into facilitation and wanted to learn from someone who was a certified facilitator. I was impatient to learn more. When one seeks, one finds!

Discovering the World of Facilitation

Yateen Gharat, through a post on the IAF WhatsApp group invited people to collaborate with him for the International Conference to be held in Tokyo. I had heard about Yateen during the Chennai conference, as the "Process Man" and the "Sticky Wall Man". I knew he was a stalwart in facilitation, and hence, I decided to take a leap of faith and called him.

It turned out to be a wise decision. During the conversation, Yateen mentioned that he conducts a program and trains facilitators. When one seeks, one finds indeed! This was just what I was looking for – an opportunity to learn in a formal way.

I got the details and decided to undergo this program and learn about facilitation in a systematic, focused way. The program was spread over 4 months; it was residential with 11 days of in-person interaction. Wow! Fortunately, I was able to take the time out and attend.

It began with the facilitators getting to know each of the participants personally. They had individual conversations with each of us to find out about our purpose and expectations, and they got to know our respective backgrounds and experience.

On the scheduled day, when I arrived at the venue, I was welcomed and greeted by Yateen. It felt really good. Over tea and breakfast, we all got to know each other, and the formal session was to start at 10.30 am. ("Create a Safe Environment).

The session started with the concept of "Being a facilitator". Honestly, this had me totally confused because I just did not understand the difference in language between "Being a facilitator" and "Doing Facilitation". I felt ashamed to voice it and kept my ignorance to myself. Mentally, I made a note that this was something I needed a clarity on[1].

---

1   I got the clarity a few days later. What they were saying was "Are you a facilitator all the time or only when you are conducting a session? Is facilitation a part of your personality?" *Dimaag ki bati jal gayi*! Now I had a lens through which I needed to see myself and my behaviour. Also, a question, when does facilitation work and when should I not use facilitation in day to day life? Where and when have I used facilitation in my life? Questions, questions, questions!

During the training, various processes were used. Some I was familiar with and others were new. The one that really stayed with me was ORID. ORID – Objective, Reflective, Interpretive, Decisional – is a process to debrief at the end of an activity or session. It is a wonderful framework for ensuring commitment. In my training sessions I was used to asking, "What did you observe?" and then went straight to "What will you do?" The ORID framework was deeper and delved into the 'why' before the decision. I have been using it since then and have noticed the difference in the commitment to the decision.

As our training continued, I heard more phrases that were repeatedly used: "Let the inmates run the asylum", "Harvest the group wisdom", "Trust the group wisdom", "Divergence, convergence", and "Rotation and revolution" among others.

The trainer in me was so uncomfortable with the first two. If the inmates are running the asylum, and it's about group wisdom, and I am not supposed to let them know my views, then what was I doing there? Why will my client pay me? I don't think I want to be a facilitator. This is all nice in theory, but it will not work in the real world! Let's have some fun and go back to doing interactive training. That is where the money is. Then the other side of me started speaking, "Keep an open mind, maybe you need to go deeper and reflect more." Ok, Let's see. Since I have already paid and I'm here for 5 days, I might as well learn with an open mind.

We were also asked to conduct a small session and given feedback, which was very helpful. This is where clarity started to emerge on what facilitation was and what wasn't. Additionally, if I wanted to become a CPF (Certified Professional Facilitator), what would be okay or not okay for my assessment. This was the first time that I was made aware that appreciating a participant with words, body language, etc. was not okay. This was exactly what I as a trainer had been doing for 15 years – clapping, giving positive strokes, – which I thought

I needed to do to keep the participants engaged and energetic. I was now able to see the difference between training and facilitation and was slowly moving towards acquiring facilitation skills.

Another memorable learning came from the time when I was running a demo session. I had got the participants to brainstorm and put all the points on the sticky wall. They then categorized it into two categories – Pros and Cons. I asked, "Which one would you like to discuss first?" During the feedback session, Yateen pointed out that that was a great facilitative question. Yeah! The trainer in me would have said, "Let's discuss pros first and then cons". So, by curbing my natural tendency and actually asking was a huge step for me. Bit by bit, I was understanding what facilitation was, and what training was, in a very practical manner.

Listed below are some of my takeaways from the 5 days:

- Learning the importance of WoW (Ways of Working). Never bypass this.

- Understanding the IAF competencies and doing a deep dive into them. The words were starting to have meaning.

- Observing how to handle differences of opinion in a facilitative manner.

Learning – A FACILITATOR NEEDS TO BE NEUTRAL.

So, no saying "wonderful point", "I agree", or "Excellent", etc. In addition to this, a facilitator needs to be aware of their body language and remain NEUTRAL. Leaning towards a participant, going closer to one group, angle at which we stand, and even greeting them with familiarity like "So nice to see you again" are all not part of facilitator language.

Another major learning was about PROCESS. In my discussion with Yateen, I asked him why so much stress on learning process.

His advice: Focus **on the desired outcome**. Choose the appropriate process. The number of processes you know is not important, but the fact that you are able to select the right process to get the desired outcome is more important. Create your own process to get the outcome. Only now it started to fall into place, and I was at peace. This was the advice from the 'Process Man'.

Those 5 days were a turning point in my journey towards understanding facilitation and "Being a Facilitator". The training continued over the next 3 months. The days of discovering the world of facilitation were wonderful.

Diving Head on

Now that I had begun to understand PROCESS and FACILITATION, I was looking at the next step. If I have a process, when should I use it and when should I not use it? What were the points that I need to keep in mind while deciding on an appropriate process? What could be some variations of the process? And what tips could some of the people who have already used it give us?

I then decided to conduct a session for the IAF Bangalore hub. The topic I chose was "FACILITATORS' TOOL KIT".

The session was announced and there were 28 registrations. WOW! Normal attendance (at that time) in the Bangalore hub events was around 18–20. Looking at the list of participants, I had butterflies. What value will these highly experienced people get from my session? How do I add value? What if they don't learn anything new? Over 3 hours of their time wasted?

At 8.30 am, all set for the session, room set, handouts placed neatly, ready to say hello to the participants as they enter. The tiny butterflies had started to take wings. I was sure everyone could see them, and they were going to emerge from some part of my body. Then the phrases came back **"Let the inmates run the asylum"**, **"trust the group wisdom"** and **"trust the process"**. I took deep breaths and repeating these phrases internally, I took the plunge.

What happened next was truly magical! The inmates ran the asylum, the group wisdom was amazing, and the process ran itself. I was stunned! Eureka! So, this is what the experienced facilitators had been telling me all along. A day that I will never forget. It was FACILITATION NIRVANA. I would wish that everyone has these moments when everything just falls into place and you can see the light.

The "inmates" experienced 11 processes in 3 hours and did a deep dive into 5 processes. DESIRED OUTCOME: ACHIEVED.

LEARNING: The realization that all those doubts and insecurities that I had, came from my trainer mindset. The questions I should have been asking myself were "How do I ensure that I harvest the group wisdom?" and "How do I ensure that everyone gets to participate?" and so on. Actually, I should have just kept the IAF competencies in front of me and gone by them. That would have been enough.

Facilitation to the rescue

Another memorable incident was with a client where I was required to conduct a training program for senior management.

I was called in to conduct a 2-day training for a client on Interviewing Skills. HR and Head of TA (Talent Acquisition) of that organization felt it was a much-needed skill. Most of the participants would be Senior management and had been conducting interviews for close to 15 years – some of them even conducting as many as 20–30 interviews a month. Knowing the participant profile, I had anticipated that the acceptance for the program may not be there. And my gut was right. So how do I get the buy in and make it a success? Facilitation to the rescue!

The first half of Day 1 was pure Facilitation. Slowly, I led them from where they were to where they would like to be. What were their challenges? How could we overcome those challenges? Needless to say, one of the solutions was to hire better people. Whose responsibility? Was it only TA? HR? No. Then do we need these skills and how are we leading our teams to hire better? By lunch time they had all agreed to and signed up for the training session.

The next 1.5 days were a breeze. The assessments subsequent to completion of training were also received with an open mind. Having won over the senior management, it resulted in 4 more batches and over 100 employees being trained.

I was thankful that I had Facilitation in my toolkit and was able to use it. I believe it is a skill every leader should have in their toolkit, to pick up and use appropriately.

The world of online facilitation

Just when I was getting comfortable with the sticky walls, colored paper, props and in-person facilitation, the world changed! It felt like the universe seems to be conspiring to keep pushing me out of my comfort zone. I'm sure you know what I am talking about. Yes, Covid-19. How does one conduct a facilitative session in a virtual world? This was a whole new stage.

I had stayed away from social media, and other forms of technology so far. My approach to technology had always been:

the less, the better, and learn the minimum required. Now, I had no choice. I needed to learn and learn quickly.

The first month of the lockdown was when I attended webinars and online sessions every day and sometimes 2–3 in a day. I was eager to learn what tools/techniques were being used and what I could use. To my surprise, almost anything that we did during in-person sessions was possible in the virtual world. I decided to get familiar with the various platforms (Zoom, Webex, MS Teams), and tools (mentimeter, mural, miro, etc.) and learn how/when to use them.

The next step was to make it a seamless experience for the participants. This meant making transitions to mentimeter or other programs smooth and giving instructions that everyone could understand. Another aspect of seamless execution was the understanding and co-ordination between the co-facilitators and the technical support. Last and not least was, of course, the discussion of what all can go wrong and how we would handle it.

Here is what we learnt:

- Putting the link for the mentimeter in the chat box, was the most seamless. Embedding the link in the actual presentation to show results created a better experience. A number of facilitators were asking participants to go to menti.com and type in the code. This usually creates confusion with people forgetting the code and it having to be repeated numerous times.

- Next, were the discussion and agreements made with the co-facilitator and the technical support. As I put myself in the position of the technical support and made a checklist of the points, I was amazed at all the things that need to be thought of. To name a few – time of entry of participants, muting audio/video, slide management, break out rooms, instructions and assignment, duration etc. What I thought would be a 15-minute conversation, actually took about 2 hours.

- Another major learning was, that as a facilitator you should know the basic technical aspects and be prepared for loss of connectivity. During one session, I was the host and the technical support. The session was being conducted by 2 co-facilitators. An hour into the session, I lost connectivity. The host privileges were assigned to the co-host and they did not realize this. After reconnecting, I needed to be made host again. How do I get this message across? We had not considered this scenario while planning! Are they even aware that I have been disconnected and have now re-joined? Desperation and BP going high. It was almost time for the breakout rooms. Who is going to create and manage it? The main facilitator did not know how to do this. Panic, panic, panic. I decided to call on the mobile. No answer. This had to be a seamless experience for the participants, there should be no break or gaps in the flow. Determined, I tried once again, and this time, the mobile was answered. Phew, just in time. Happy to say that the participants did not experience any disruption and had no clue to what happened "behind the scenes".

- Tremendous learning. Especially after conducting so many in person sessions, we were all familiar with the 'what to do to get it right' and knew how to anticipate/handle those situations. This was a whole new world, with new challenges. Really throwing me out into deep virtual waters. Today I am comfortable conducting engaging sessions and using technology. Of course, the learning on different platforms continues.

- Conducting and attending numerous sessions over the past few months, has reinforced for me the importance of preparation. As an experienced facilitator has shared, "to run a great facilitative session – 80% is pre work, 10% is delivery and 10% is post session evaluation". So true! To conduct a 2-hour session, took more than 80 hours of preparation.

Here and now

My journey continues, so much to learn and practice. The journey towards "BEING" a facilitator has been exciting. Along the way I have met some wonderful, generous co-travellers who have made this journey very pleasant. We continue traveling together. Destination: "BEING" a facilitator.

Desired Outcome

Sushma Banthia

Are facilitation skills acquired? Are some of us facilitators and unaware that we are using facilitation? I was having this conversation with one of my mentors and he asked me a question, "When did you first use facilitation?" This got me thinking and it took me down memory lane and stopped in 1969.

St Agnes Loreto, Lucknow. I was in class 6. My father had been transferred to Lucknow and I was new to the school. Academically, I was very good and at the top of the class and hence the teacher's favourite. Also being a whiz at maths, I would finish the assignments in about 10 minutes and had the rest of the time to either finish my homework or help my teacher with some task. Undoubtedly, I was a teacher's pet.

What about my classmates? Different story here. I certainly was not getting positive vibes on that front. I got to know that they considered me dominating and I was not their favorite person. Why? What had I done to deserve this? I found one classmate who was slightly sympathetic and decided to talk to her outside the school premises. She gave me the same feedback, that I was dominating. Puzzled, I requested her to give me an example for me to understand better. "Well, think of the lunch break. You always decide the game we are to play. You never ask us." What to me was confidence was being perceived as dominance. Ok, so I learnt my lesson. ASK don't TELL. Ask everyone, hold your own ideas, get consensus. Divergence to convergence. When I consciously started practicing that, everything changed. This was the first instance that I can remember where I used facilitation and what a change it made.

Learning: Listen, get everybody's ideas/thoughts, get convergence, get consensus, go forward.

A very powerful leadership lesson learnt on the playing field, which contributed to my success in the corporate sector.

Facilitation as a Leader

Let me now share why I keep saying that facilitation is an essential leadership tool, especially in today's business environment. This is from the time when I was employed at Cook Pacemaker Corporation, USA. I joined the Engineering Department as a programmer and was the junior most person in the Engineering Department.

At Cook, we were working on pacemaker models which needed to get into production ASAP. The projects were behind schedule. The team working on the pacemaker project was a multidisciplinary team of 15: Electronic Engineers, Electrical Engineers, Mechanical Engineer, Firmware Specialist, Computer Programmers, and Technicians. Due to various reasons, the position of Head of Department was kept vacant and 4 of the senior Engineers reported to the President. It was a dysfunctional team. Hence, the project was already delayed by over a year by the time I joined. Also, being a life-saving device, no bugs were acceptable in the code or in its functioning. FDA approval had not been obtained.

To cut a long story short, 5 months after joining, I was offered the responsibility of the project and position of the Head of Department, Engineering. This came as a surprise to me and the rest of the company. There were a number of senior employees who felt that the President was making a huge mistake, while others felt that I was the scapegoat and being setup to take the fall for the delay in the project. Some even advised me to watch out.

I was called into the conference room. The President and the Vice President (Finance) were there. It was a short conversation, after which the President told the VP that he was making me responsible for the pacemaker project and offering me the position of Head of Department. Till today I remember his response and that conversation so clearly. The VP said to the President, "We have tried so many times, and no one has succeeded in that position. What makes you think she will succeed?"

The reply from President was short, "Everybody listens to her, she can get the job done." That was it. It was now up to me, and I decided to accept the challenge.

Back in my cubicle, I reflected on that conversation: "Everybody listens to her. She can get the job done." **The truth was that I listened to everyone, understood their perspectives, and got consensus.** A lesson learnt during my school days. **Without knowing it and without any formal training in facilitation, I was using facilitation skills.**

Having accepted the responsibility, I got to work. With the help of my team, I started understanding the entire project, learnt project management techniques, and planned our way forward. I also learnt the meaning of statements like, "You can't test quality into a product, you have to build quality into it." No amount of testing was going to make it a quality product that we as a company could have confidence in. Six months later, I decided to inform the President, in writing, that we as a Department, felt that this product, with the current code, could not be released into the market.

All hell broke loose. The owner, Mr. Bill Cook flew down, while the President, the Vice President were let go. Mr. Cook then called me and asked me whether we could do this project and what we would need. I told him that it could be done and all I needed was permission to start all over again. I was given a free hand and 4 months. I had only 4 months to get it done.

How do I get everyone to work as a team? Everyone was needed and we had to succeed. Without wasting time, I got everyone into the conference room.

First step: **Desired outcome.** We had to build a quality product in 4 months.

How were we going to do this? How were we going to work together? How were we going to communicate with the other departments?

I asked these questions of the team and let them decide. This wonderful co-creation took a few days and we finally had a plan. All the ways of working were co-created. Every member of the team felt safe to contribute and express their ideas, they felt that their voice mattered, there was ownership and accountability, roles were defined and the work started. It was their plan. My role – I facilitated, asked, did not give my opinion, just set the desired outcome.

This dysfunctional team was now finally becoming a proper team and working together. Work was progressing well. The turnaround was amazing. The same set of people were now so energized, the project was moving forward at a good pace. The respect for the Engineering Department rose in the eyes of the other departments and in the company.

As a leader, I was using the skill of facilitation, even though I was not aware of it.

We had until December 31. By the last week of November, it was clear that we would be ready for an evaluation. We had completed the project early – in just 3 months! Mind boggling. If this had been done from the start, the product would have been out in the market and the huge loss could have been avoided. And all this had happened, with the same set of people! No one from Engineering was fired or hired. The only thing that had changed was the method. The entire team was involved, there was co-creation, and ask not tell. The entire company had confidence in our team and the product now. They had observed how we had worked.

It is experiences like this that have made me a big fan of facilitation. **One must urge every leader and project manager to learn and apply this skill and experience the power of facilitation. You will get a quality product in a timely manner, with a high performing team.**

So where I am now? I formally learnt about facilitation 5 years back. I have learnt to refer to the International Association of Facilitators (IAF) competencies, understand them better, focus on desired outcome, choosing the process carefully and appropriately. Learning to stay neutral and asking rather than telling. Have a better understanding of trainer mindset vs facilitator mindset. Attempting at BEING a Facilitator.

Having the understanding of the differences between teaching, training, mentoring and facilitation has helped me consciously choose the appropriate technique. Ultimately, it is all about the Desired Outcome.

Yateen Gharat (CPF)

Yateen Gharat is Certified Professional Facilitator, Outbound Facilitator, Leadership Development coach, NLP Master trainer, and MBTI for the past 20 years. Some of the hats he wears are Facilitator, Trainer, Coach, Survival expert, Mountaineer, Rock climber and Endurance cyclist. Yateen help teams in making conversations meaningful using a variety of tools from his repertoire. He works with Leadership teams from across the world for OD, Strategic planning, and in the people development arena. He spends about 20% of his work time doing community and NGO work. Yateen is trusted for his commitment towards holistic change.

The Facilitation Expedition

Yateen Gharat

Who am I?

I am Yateen Gharat, popularly known as an outdoor adventure survival expert. I started my journey in facilitation way back in 2012 and I'm a Certified Professional Facilitator (CPF), an outbound facilitator for 21 years and a trained mountaineer.

My Background

My curiosity had me spend most of my training days in mountains and campsites that enriched me with immense learnings and unforgettable experiences. I have seamlessly incorporated this wealth of knowledge and experience in the training programs for the corporate, especially in team building and leadership development.

Outdoor Management Development Methodology was a gift from my mountain excursions from some of our senior mountaineer colleagues. 1997 was the year when I started conducting outbound facilitation, using the experiential learning methodology and since then there has been no stopping.

The experiential learner in me always pushed me to experiment with new techniques resulting in a highly effective session. As they say, one picture can portray thousand words; so, does one small experience that has been debriefed well convey a learning worth million-words in the shortest possible time.

Concurrently, I continued to hone my skills as an experiential educator by working as a visiting faculty in a top management college and have conducted about 140 workshops of 2 days each for almost 4 years. One of the significant outcomes of this experience has been that I learned to be more flexible and be open for diverse outcomes, which is an important skill for being an effective facilitator.

First Experience of Facilitation

TISS – Tata Institute of Social Sciences, where I attended my first session on facilitation, was the beginning of my journey as a group process facilitator.

I still remember how the session started and the two facilitators present in the room with a calm, poised and a very welcoming demeanour. Instead of teaching something, they asked us to write what we wanted to learn on a post-it and stick it up on the wall. I started to wonder why they were not teaching us anything and rather asking us this question. Post this activity, we were given an hour's break and I was really curious as to why this session had not started yet, and what was the need for a break!

To my amazement, once the break got over and the facilitators came back, something radical happened. I was still unsure on what was going to happen next. This was when the facilitators welcomed us back in the room and announced that based on the participants' inputs on the learning expectations, they had designed the program for next 5 days.

Now this was absolutely new and also a bit shocking to me!

Well, so far, any training program I had witnessed was typically agenda and slide show driven, but what had happened at TISS was so different from anything I had experienced before. And of course, the curiosity in me could not wait to see how this experience would unfold.

At this point in time, I was unaware of the exact meaning and definition of Group Process Facilitation. The next 5 days were unequivocally facilitated where the participants had assumed the centre stage. All the participants expressed as many ideas and views they could, we held a lot of discussions, and the facilitators were around only as little as required with very little to no intervention. This was a rather strange and different experience for me.

The Rendezvous of my Mental Acquisitiveness

My inquiring mind with a first of its kind experience at Tata Institute of Social Sciences had generated a keen interest and a quest to know more about facilitation and its workings. Those 5 days had me connect to myself as I participated and in particular what I enjoyed the most was that the facilitators did not impose their viewpoints on any of us. I felt heard, I was included, and the outcomes were a result of my expectations.

The satisfaction of attending this workshop was tremendous. For first time in my experience, out of the many training workshops from the past that I had attended, I was allowed to express myself with complete freedom. This was just what I wanted. The whole situation was revolving around the participants, which was really intriguing about Group Process facilitation.

The Unparalleled Experience of Facilitation with IAF India

I met Vinay Kumar, the facilitator, at a session conducted by International Association of Facilitators (IAF) India – Mumbai. This was way back in 2013 and I was invited by a colleague to attend this session.

Having heard of the IAF community previously, which had a reputation, I had high expectations of the session and I was looking forward for yet another rich experience, but I had kept my mind open. I reached the conference venue before time, and facilitators were busy setting up the room but greeted me with a smile.

Vinay was candid when he spoke to us. He did not use a microphone, nor a slideshow. People were sitting around the table in a clustered manner when he came in and introduced himself. He conducted an activity for delegates to introduce themselves to others. It was chaos but filled with enthusiasm as everyone present in the room was interacting with each other and by the end of 15 minutes we almost got to know half the participants in the room personally.

That energy transitioned into another process which was equally engaging and I kept waiting for the facilitator to start speaking and teaching but that never happened. Throughout the session we would be in some group for some process and then we would find ourselves in another group while the time was flying really fast. I didn't even realise that it was lunch time as by then we had done some enormous amount of work as a group. My memory of the facilitator was that he moved around while keeping an unobtrusive eye on the events while we worked as a group, and he would crack jokes, have casual conversations, but never did I see him take a control of the proceedings. In a way his absence was felt in his presence.

The unforgettable sight of the group's involvement in activities and processes, colourful chart papers, colour markers, oil pastels and some really astounding stationary and of course my first rendezvous with the Sticky Wall (the Magic wall on which the coloured papers would stick automatically!) was truly enchanting.

Through the day, as the work progressed in all the groups, the walls kept filling up with chart papers prepared by the teams and eventually by the end of the day, everyone gathered around these walls looking up at the work produced on these chart papers by all the teams. And soon after, we found ourselves giving team presentations on the ideas that were so creatively expressed on these chart papers, as everything was handwritten. So many colours were exciting, and all of it was looking so enthralling when we were hearing the other groups present. The learnings from each other were so immense and there it was – 5 o'clock – when we were about to close the session, but with a strange realization that we have learnt so much but nothing has been taught to us in a conventional way.

What was really intriguing, was the methodology rather than the topic of discussion. I really couldn't comprehend what I was experiencing.

Vinay gleefully asked us, "So, guys, please tell me which part from this collective knowledge up on the wall is really taught by me?"

While the crowd said in unison, "You actually taught us nothing, we simply co-created the whole learning", he smiled graciously!

A true revelation was that a facilitator did not teach yet all the people in the group were engaged, involved and they could create truly meaningful outcomes for themselves and people learning from each other. There was no teaching and yet the learning was immense.

That's where I said to myself, this is novel, engaging, inclusive and it creates a great sense of satisfaction in the end! A decision was made at that very moment to pursue and follow Group Process Facilitation and I joined the IAF community as a member and my journey as a facilitator started there.

My interest continued to grow leaps and bounds with a drive to take initiative and grow towards the chosen path after attending every session at the IAF. During my first IAF experience everything appeared so magical, yet there was a science behind it! I continued to question myself on what the way forward was to learn this methodology.

This quest led me to embark on a true exploration of Group Process Facilitation methodology.

As the magic of facilitation continued a new journey had begun

The empowering journey had started as I got associated with the IAF India, Mumbai chapter. It was amazing to experience different facilitators at various sessions conducted by IAF. I witnessed magic and got hooked on to the art of facilitation. Tools like sticky wall, coloured papers, and chiselled markers were even more fascinating.

Every time I attended a session at IAF I could sense a change in my state of mind from a person who is always in a rush and engrossed in the life's hustle and bustle, to a person who connects with a larger purpose, a big picture through meaningful associations with everyone present.

As I witnessed different facilitators who presented their new techniques and processes, the experience was only something that could be felt and not expressed in words.

Apparently, I did realise that there is a science behind all this magic and it's not as easy as it appears. I had already started exploring, reading and experimenting the facilitation methodology in my outbound and training sessions with some unseen and amazing results. The experimental learning, research and development with facilitation methodology continued till 2014. Finally, I decided that in order to reach at the peak of knowing all about facilitation, it was important to embark on a journey to get a CPF certification from the International Association of Facilitators (IAF).

CPF means a Certified Professional Facilitator. I started gathering information, sought support from existing CPFs and that is when I realised that in 2014, India had only 2–3 CPFs.

My reasons to pursue this journey was twofold. Firstly, everything about facilitation felt magical and secondly, it would be a tough, challenging journey which would make it even more worthwhile to achieve. The learning would be staunch.

Being a trekker and a mountaineer all my life, it is extremely thrilling and exciting to accomplish the most difficult and challenging tasks which usually gives me a sense of drive and passion.

The captivating obsession for facilitation – Why?

I knew an enthralling long journey had begun as I experimented with my observations at various IAF sessions and a deep dive into the methodology of Group Process Facilitation.

It typically takes about three years to prepare, learn and conduct sessions, to understand facilitation on your own. A worrisome thought nudged me on being able to get a certification with just 2 years of exposure. But deep within I knew I could accomplish this.

What followed was not only to observe sessions for my learnings as a facilitator but also practising facilitation at every available opportunity, which was not restricted to IAF sessions but also extended to commercial assignments. I still remember the first opportunity to practise facilitation commercially and it was supposed to be a motivational session with a time frame of 2 hours. I was about to reject the offer via an email stating that I am not a motivational speaker but rather would love to conduct an experiential learning team bonding activity.

Something stopped me from doing that though and instead, I arranged a call with the client to explain to them all about facilitation and the various possibilities it can generate. I got a chance to visit the client, understand their requirements and explain what I had up my sleeve to offer!

To be on the safe side, I sent them two proposals later that evening. One with engaging activities and another with a full-fledged facilitation process plan. Voila! They loved the idea of engaging 65 people meaningfully by using group process facilitation.

My first session – I had the jitters and unsure of how it would go. All I had was a clear vision, as I had done my homework well. It was beyond my imagination to handle 65 people in the first go. I started the process, and took the plunge by trusting myself and my instincts. I was personally astonished and the power of facilitation was unbelievable.

The participants, oblivious of the passing time were deeply engrossed, and when I announced it was time for me to conduct the debrief and close the session, they negotiated and with a request from the management had the session extended and agenda changed for the day.

A sense of deep satisfaction prevailed as I experienced the sheer magic and power of facilitation. I had it engraved within me by this time that my future lies in facilitation. It will be a way of life for me, to use group facilitation to help organisations, teams and communities.

The challenges I faced and choices I made to become a CPF

"Always go with the choice that scares you most, because that's the one that is going to help you grow,"

– Caroline Myss

Facilitation was a new concept in India, and it was becoming difficult for me to talk to someone and offer a facilitation program instead of a conventional training workshop. In 2014, most people seemed to believe that facilitation, training, and coaching are all interchangeable terms and any of these terms encompass all of these ideas.

Multiple attempts to explain people that facilitation is different were made but something did not strike well with them during these discussions. It was important for me to have conducted a certain number of sessions in order to fit the eligibility criteria for applying for the CPF Certificate. Hence, I had to change my approach from trying to convince the clients to allow me to conduct facilitation sessions. I started to seek the client's permission to give me the freedom to use any methodology of my choice to achieve the desired outcome and surprisingly they would agree. The clients started to see results and opened up to my methodology of facilitation.

That was my first breakthrough in terms of how I would approach any client request and use group process facilitation. I converted all the opportunities for trainings, content facilitation and the outbound workshops to group process facilitation. I realised that facilitation can work and would always work in any situation. In person, I am yet to come across a situation where facilitation did not work!

Eventually, I managed to get around 26 opportunities to facilitate before I could apply for the CPF assessment.

The application for CPF requires some serious documentation. My application got accepted, and I was excited with an even more powerful desire and paid up the fees which was almost about US $1000 in 2014. After the acceptance of my application, a powerful 3-months journey with IAF assessors commenced.

My Journey through the World of Facilitation

> *"Remember to celebrate the milestones as you prepare for the road ahead."*
>
> **– Nelson Mandela**

The very first milestone, as I started to learn about facilitation, was, *You know it when you know it*. The clearest and purest form of group process facilitation. I realised that for the magical appearance of a facilitated process or session, a lot of hard work and planning is needed way before the actual session begins.

It was extremely fulfilling to be able to put every learning I had into practice. From my experience of being an experiential educator I realised I was also a pragmatic learner. I learnt deeply by doing things and reflecting on them, which enhanced my facilitation skills throughout.

- The first milestone I wanted to achieve was to gain a deep knowledge and understanding of everything there was about the theory of facilitation.
- The Second milestone was to practice adequately to validate the theory that I understood.
- The Third milestone was to apply for a certified professional facilitation certification process by IAF.
- The Fourth milestone was to get through with the certification assessment process.
- Ultimately, I managed to pass the CPF assessment in 2015, Mumbai, India.

Getting certified was not the end, though. In fact, it was the inception of my journey as a certified group process facilitator. I must admit, one can never know everything about group facilitation, and it is always a work-in-progress.

The certification, however, gave me a boost and I enjoyed using facilitation in various complex situations and it was a way of challenging my own understanding of facilitation. To my surprise, every time I would end up knowing more about facilitation. The more I practised, the more I learnt.

Around 2016, I realised that to know and learn more I may want to teach facilitation. My firm belief is you teach utmost of what you want to learn to the fullest. That's how I started a pioneering program named Train The Facilitator (TTF Gold) to teach group process facilitation! This was the first ever open facilitation skills program offered in India.

It was a three-month program in which participants would undergo five days of intense training. It consisted of two days of learning processes, three days of practicing and two more days for assessment – a total of 12 days of face to face training spread across 3 months.

The backbone of this workshop were these simple questions:

1. What is group process facilitation?
2. What is the role of a facilitator?
3. What are the different processes?
4. What are the applications?

Since then, I have conducted 24 batches of the TTF workshop. The diversity of participants in each group has brought me new learnings on facilitation each time, further deepening my knowledge.

Tata Institute of Social Sciences approached me in the year 2019 to conduct a similar program under their banner for the Centre for Lifelong Learning branch. I agreed immediately and since then we have been conducting two batches of 5 days each year. The program with TISS is light and a basic level program. A certificate of participation is given to all the participants.

During this fruitful journey, a conscious discernment dawned upon me to work with NGOs and an environment for community development as facilitation skills would make a huge difference in their environment and this thought made me divide my work into two parts. Today I do about 50% of commercial assignments and 50% NGO work.

The best part about NGO work is, it gives you an immense sense of fulfilment and satisfaction.

Keep your eyes on the stars and your feet on the ground

Looking back on my achievements, it is fair to say that I am extremely proud of what I have done and accomplished so far. My major focus areas have been to conduct as many as possible facilitation interventions in the corporates, work for NGOs and do community work, and teach facilitation skills.

The obsession I have with facilitation has been growing ever since with an enhancement of facilitation skills as well. With a sense of pride, I would love to mention about my ability to design 40 group facilitation processes. I have always believed in giving back to the community and I plan to write a book on these processes in the near future, for an easy access to everyone out there who want to make a difference.

The processes I have designed have been getting selected by IAF in the international as well as India conferences to be presented. In 2019, I was also invited by IAF China to present a process to the upcoming community in there.

I have presented in the Taiwan conference, the Korea conference, the Malaysia conference and a process designed by me also got selected in the Japan conference as well as the 2020 IAF Global Summit. Unfortunately, I could not reach Japan due to typhoon and the Global Summit 2020 has been postponed due to the pandemic.

Ever since the CPF Certification, I have consistently presented in all India conferences – Bangalore, Delhi, Pune and Chennai. I have consistently presented for the IAF Global webinars at least twice a year. I have been associated with IAF India and the Mumbai core team hub. This gives me a chance to conduct mentoring sessions for Aspiring Facilitators.

In association with the ongoing IAF Global mentorship program in 2019, I have mentored 5 aspiring facilitators, while this year I am mentoring 2 aspiring facilitators.

While working and improving on my Facilitation skills since 2014, I have also been an active part of Institute of Cultural affairs ICA India. ICA methods are known as Technology of Participation (ToP) methods across the world and they are very helpful for community development. For the first couple of years I learnt these methods and processes, namely ORID, Consensus Workshop Method, Participatory Strategic Planning Method, Wall of Wonder Method, Imaginal Change Method, Design Eye Method, Social Process Method, the Spirit of Facilitation Method, and the Facilitating Client Collaboration Method, to name a few.

After couple a of years of learning these methods, I started co-training with ICI India director Shankar Jadhav. It was a blessing and an immense pleasure to learn from Shankar Jadhav who comes with 4 decades of experience.

It has been a power packed journey of teaching what I learn and learning what I teach thus far, which has made my facilitation skills even more robust. And I'm grateful for the all the opportunities that only keep coming my way and helping me grow.

The Covid Saga

Yateen Gharat

I reside on the outskirts of the Mumbai – Mira Road, in the district of Thane and in my Colony, the reaction of the people was of that of apprehension and sheer anxiety when the lockdown was imposed on 22nd March 2020 in Mumbai. We were trying to console each other by saying that this would last for a maximum of 30 days or maybe two months or so and that we will be back to our normal life in no time. What we didn't know at that time was that the pandemic and ensuing lockdown would go on for more than six months. In fact, lockdown restrictions and the fear of contracting Corona were still alive then, barely after a week of official lockdown announcement. Everything outside was appearing grim and dull, no one was venturing out and slowly, a situation came that the supplies of essentials started running out for a few houses and then we started seeing people cautiously beginning to move about to procure essentials. And then came the news that there was someone in our colony, from building number 8, who had tested positive for the Covid-19 virus. It was evident that as per government measures, the authorities would close down the entire Colony.

My colony consists of 28 buildings and we predicted a very strict lockdown, meaning that all the three access gates would be sealed, and no one would be able to move out nor could an outsider come inside our colony.

This is when I really started thinking fast. I predicted that for at least 14 days we would be cut off from the outside world, which was already paralysed! The anxiety and fear were evident in the faces of the residents. What would happen now? Were we all going to contract the Coronavirus? Will it spread across all the buildings?

While these were the primary thoughts of most people, no one was saying it out loud yet.

In that moment, as a facilitator, I realised that this was the time I had to do something, and I decided to call upon the secretaries of all the 28 buildings. After we gathered in the garden area, we stood within the circle and I asked them these questions:

- What does it look Like?
- What do you think? What may we do for the colony?
- What are your concerns?
- What are the proposed solutions?
- What action can we take?

There was deafening silence for about 2 minutes. Then, they started talking. Some of them they could not articulate well, but since a chance was given for everyone to speak, together we came up with what our immediate reaction to this situation should be first. As the ideas were flowing in, I was documenting all of them on my tablet.

Once all the ideas were expressed, I asked them to choose the best that would work for the entire colony, which was followed by a deep and heavy discussion about possible implementation.

Soon, some action plans were finalized with an agreement that we need to assess the situation every day and we would need to course correct our action plans accordingly. Then, one of the secretaries casually said that if we could have this kind of discussion during our committee meetings, the results of the meetings would be different! The others smiled in an agreement. It had been a different experience for all of them as everybody was allowed to talk and many innovative ideas were coming as I was taking notes on my tablet.

The first thing decided during the group discussion was to form a task force. Then the channel for the communication was decided: a WhatsApp group of the task force. Some secretaries already had a WhatsApp group for their respective buildings and those secretaries who did not have one, committed to making one before that evening. That was to monitor the all-pervasive communication as well as a group for volunteers – 4 people from each building would be volunteering.

Now that the groundwork and preparation was completed, we now had to think about how to procure supplies! Someone suggested, why not get the vendor for essentials inside the colony itself and settle him down in the open garden area! Almost instantly, everyone agreed and the work started immediately, and by that evening we had finalized on the vendors for milk, vegetables, groceries, fruits, and other miscellaneous items.

Overnight, all the vendors were established inside the colony and none of our colony members had to venture out of the colony during those 15 days of the lockdown period, which then incidentally got extended to 36 days.

People still thank me and thank the entire team with this initiative because the fear of coronavirus during that time was really high. In fact, some people were thinking that they might get coronavirus even by just venturing out of the house and there were many myths that were making the rounds on the news channels. Those were the times when media and social media were disturbing the sanity and peace of mind of all the people. There was fear of the unknown in the air.

In retrospection, I realized that so many people had benefited just because I had been able to gather these people together and

I had used facilitation methodologies to implement what was critically needed at that juncture.

The implementation from my side as a facilitator looked something like this:

- Sensing the need of collective
- Generating data about the real needs of the colony residents
- Gathering data about the special needs of some elderly and less able people (physically and financially)
- Getting thought leaders together for possible action
- Facilitating the discussion about consensus for what to do and prioritize
- Delegation of various activities
- Monitoring in the initial phase and applying course correction in relevant areas

My learnings from this exercise:

- It's easy to get diverse minds together when the deliverables and the noble cause is clear.
- The emergent was a bit difficult to handle, yet with teamwork it was managed well.
- Keeping an eye and ear open for listening to the needs of people – stated as well as unstated.
- Most importantly, once a group is aligned to the 'Why' of the Noble cause and the service, they are much better off and feel more motivated and empowered from within than a single leader dictating the deliverables.

Nasreen Khan

Nasreen is an optimistic and empathetic human being. She brings simplicity, authenticity, and commitment to whatever she chooses to do. As a Coach and Facilitator, she supports both individuals and organizations to be their best. With three decades of experience, Nasreen has learnt the importance of balancing the philosophical with the practical. The mysteries of the human mind also fascinate her. Nasreen loves the mountains, travels extensively and is an ardent nature lover.

Nuts, Bolts, and Jolts

Nasreen Khan

The three-hour flight to Chennai had been turbulent. In the last half an hour, the passengers' prayers had also become more audible. It was still pouring heavily when I landed. It felt good to be on steady ground. Intermittent streaks of lightning lit up the dark sky, giving a glimpse of water-laden clouds. Despite the grim weather forecast, I had decided to travel. I was going to attend a conference that had been highly recommended.

This was the annual conference for facilitators. Despite the rain, the conference seemed to have full attendance. For two days, from 8.30 am till 6.30 pm, I had found myself in and out of sessions. In each session, I had explored a different topic with a new group and with different facilitators. It had been a good experience, but it had also been quite overwhelming for me.

I was now at the closing plenary. The facilitators conducting this last session gave us time to stop and reflect on the two days gone by. They asked us to share with one other person, what we were taking away from the conference.

The young man I had partnered with had recently joined the training profession. He was an enthusiastic and inquisitive learner. He asked me what my biggest learning from the conference had been. I was unable to find one specific one to share, but I told him that it seemed to have shifted something inside me. That made him curious. He shot several quick questions at me. He wanted to know what that shift was! He wanted to know about my journey. How had

I started? What brought me to facilitation? And most importantly, how had I learnt facilitation? What would I advise him?

As I began to think of the answers to his questions, my mind went back to many years ago, when I had got my first job.

I started my career, as most MBA graduates do, with a campus placement in a corporate. I was in hardcore sales – doing prospecting, cold calls, daily targets, monthly targets, and all that goes into making sales happen! After working for a few years with a couple of organizations, I decided to become an entrepreneur. In 1995, I set up a recruitment firm in Delhi, called Catalysts.

A friend and I ran the business for over 15 years. During this time, we built lasting relationships with our customers – candidates and clients. I noticed that two parts of my work gave me immense joy: one was the conversations I had with clients, helping them clarify their needs, the second was supporting candidates prepare for their interviews. Going by the referrals we got, clients and candidates seemed to love the work we did too. I would get a high when someone who had been previously struggling was able to crack an interview!

Soon, I started getting requests for running training sessions on interviewing skills. I would take on these with delight, burning the midnight oil to deliver practical inputs that seemed to get good results.

It was extremely fulfilling to help people grow and develop. But recruitment was what I knew and what I was particularly good at. It was also what earned me my living. I had no experience in training. Jumping into unknown waters and re-starting as a novice in a new area, after 15 years of a steady and successful venture? That sounded both scary and foolish.

As they say, if something excites and scares you at the same time, you should do it.

I got my first large training project from an engineering college based in Sonipat, near Delhi. I was to conduct sessions on 'personal development' for over nine hundred students. This gave me a great chance to learn and practice. For over two years, I continued to offer these sessions to engineering and MBA colleges across NCR. Gradually, I also started getting opportunities in corporate organizations and NGOs for conducting training in other areas as well.

I would put in days and days of preparation before a single session. From the very generous resources on Google, I would access the theories available on the subject. I would study how other trainers had explored a topic, watch TED talks & videos, and scan through hundreds of articles. It was endless. For every session, I made copious notes, sometimes running into a notebook. I would also shortlist 25–30 PowerPoint presentations that I would thoroughly study. It was then that I would design my own PowerPoint presentation, around which I would run the sessions. It was intense work, but it taught me a lot.

To begin with, all my training sessions were delivered around this well-researched PowerPoint, with some activities thrown in for engagement and practice. Somewhere along the journey, as the audience changed, (and I changed!) the style of delivery also changed. The PowerPoint was now thrown in occasionally. It was activities and games that dominated the sessions. Something else seemed to have taken centerstage.

I began attending programs with different trainers to learn from them. I explored a variety of topics like communication, leadership, motivation, presentation skills, etc. It was amazing to see the unique styles and knowledge the trainers had. I would come back and make notes of what I liked (and did not!). There was a lot to learn.

During this exploration, I got the chance to attend a "train the trainer" program in Delhi. Conducted by Thomas Goldthorp, the three days were full of fun and learning.

I discovered that while Thomas had a PowerPoint, he did not use it at all during the sessions! He used it only during breaks to show some quotations. We had flip charts all around the room, and he used those when he needed to explain a concept. I learnt more from the activities that we did in groups, than from the theory he shared. He switched our groups as well, so I had a chance to interact with almost all participants in the workshop.

I observed that Thomas had an amazing knack of sensing the group's energy. If we looked energized and ready, he would introduce a theory or some tools to grapple with. If we seemed low on energy, he would take us through some game or activities, letting us discover what we needed.

I left that workshop armed with tools and confidence to last me a lifetime. *I realized that I did not need a PowerPoint to make a training work.* It was a paradigm shift in the way I had experienced training so far! Flipcharts, post-it notes, and charts took on a new meaning for me as a trainer. I became acutely aware of the collective knowledge and insights that group work brought. I also realized that games and activities could increase engagement and learning.

This program not only changed the way I delivered my training sessions, it also changed what I wanted to learn. There were new skills and knowledge that I would now go looking for.

A few months later, I learnt of Sivasailam "Thiagi" Thiagarajan, who was known to be a master in the use of games in training (I had heard that he would create one new game/activity every day to add to his collection!). He was going to be in India and would offer a program on the use of games in training. Since I was now using games very actively, this seemed to be exactly the opportunity I needed. I was certain that attending his workshop would help me design games even better. So off I went to Mumbai!

It was the first day of the workshop. We were immersed in a 'game' on anagrams at our tables. The set up was such that we were competing against the other tables. I was the leader for my table. Seeing us struggle, Thiagi came to our table and offered to give us a hint. As the leader of the team, I self-righteously refused. Our team was sure we would be able to crack it with no help, which to our joy, we did. The team that won had taken the hint offered to solve the anagram. We came second and were rejoicing in the fact that we had solved it without any help at all.

During the debrief, Thiagi looked around the room and said with a chuckle, "I also found some remarkably confident leaders who refused the hint I was offering. I wonder what stopped them from taking the hint. Nowhere in the rules did I say the hint was out of bounds." Grinning, he looked around, holding my attention a moment longer, to let me know he had noticed. In his inimitable, tongue-in-cheek style, he continued, "I wonder what these leaders do in their own lives. Do they take help? Or do they create rules that don't exist and make life difficult for themselves and for others?"

I was stunned! I had come to this program to learn how to create and use games. And here was this trainer, nudging me to become aware of a behaviour pattern I was clueless about. This was not what I had thought I would take away from the program; it was way beyond that. I realized it was not about the game or activity. *What was important were the observations a facilitator could make during the activity. Equally important was the debrief and the skill a facilitator had to play back these observations to participants for their reflection.*

From that day on, observations and debrief became key tools in my toolkit.

My training sessions were becoming more impactful. As I learnt and practiced, I was able to deliver better value to my clients. But I had only worked with small groups. I wanted to know how to work with, and impact large groups. I decided to attend a three-day train-the-trainer workshop on LSIP (Large Scale Interactive Process). This would help me learn how to manage larger group sizes.

We were 450 participants in a single, large hall. Several large TV screens were placed along the longer edges of the hall. There were 45–50 round tables, around which participants sat in groups of 8 to 10 each. Each table had a flip chart on a stand next to it and lots of marker pens. The workshop was being run by two facilitators – Anil Sachdeva and Kanti Gopal. There was also a large operations team that was managing the logistics.

During a session, Kanti gave us some simple instructions: we were to work in our 8-member group to answer a few questions. This was a 40-minute exercise. It was an engrossing set of questions. Only after 10–12 minutes had elapsed did we realize that we would like some clarity on one of the questions. This is when we looked around for the facilitators.

We could not see either of them. Since the hall was large, some of us stood up and went looking for them. We were unable to find them. Having lost some precious minutes in this, our group decided to proceed with our own understanding of the question.

This incident stayed with me. I thought it was quite unprofessional for the facilitators not to be available to answer our team's query during the exercise. (The operations and support team were there in the room, though). During lunch break, I voiced this to Kanti. He seemed to guess what I was thinking.

He asked me in his low, quiet voice, "Nasreen, was your group able to come up with answers to the questions on your table?" "Yes," I answered, "but we were unsure if we were doing what we were supposed to do. We wanted to ask one of you to be sure we were in the right direction."

"The intent of this process is to allow you to think and do what you/your group decide is right," he said. "If we had been in the room, you would have asked us and ended up doing what we think is right, not what you think is right. We would have come in the way of the process. As a facilitator, I didn't want to come in the way of the process."

Before I could ask any more questions, Kanti moved away. I would have loved to ask him more. But I figured by moving away he was once again demonstrating what he had just said. *Trusting a group enough to leave it to find its own answers.* This was an important but difficult one for me to imbibe. My struggle on this one continues!

As the years passed, I was getting more immersed into training. My ability to observe and sense individuals and groups was improving. I realized how much of a difference this single ability could make. I started exploring how I could get better at this.

Upon enquiring, several people pointed me to Neuro Linguistic Programming – more commonly called NLP. The little research I did on the subject, unfortunately, did not convince me. Since several voices pointed to a program in Bangalore being run by Ashlesh Rao, I decided to give it a try. Though I signed up for the seven-day program, I had decided I would leave midway if I did not find value in it.

But during those seven days, something changed. I went into the program as a skeptic and returned a convert!

Ashlesh was a playful, insightful, and humble facilitator. He build great rapport with each participant. His intent to support each participant shone through. He allowed each one to take (or not to take) what they wished. I realized it was his intention, authenticity, and humility that moved me. It allowed me to be open to exploring what I would have otherwise blocked out.

This was a lifelong lesson for me. I had not thought that the 'being' of a facilitator could influence a participant. But now I had experienced how it had impacted my own openness to learn. *I now understood what a critical role the 'being' of a facilitator plays in the process.*

Time flew, like it does when you love what you do. I was getting great assignments. I was getting to experiment and learn. I had added coaching tools to my kitty, and that too helped in facilitation. In the meantime, I also continued to attend training programs to keep my learning on.

I was attending one such training program. It was a two-day coaching workshop. There were only six of us, all of us being either coaches or facilitators. I was not enjoying the program at all. The trainer boasted about his achievements, he put up slide after slide that he read out verbatim, he gave us badly photocopied hand-outs, he arrived late for the sessions, he bad-mouthed other trainers. I was very put off.

If not for the fact that I was in a remote part of Noida with no transportation to go back, I would have left the program. A co-participant had promised to give me a lift to my place in Delhi, so I had to wait for him. As I sat in my colleague's car to go home, I remarked "this was such a waste of time and money!"

My assumption was, that like me, my colleague would also not have got any value from the program.

"Actually, I learnt a lot," he said. I looked at him to be sure he wasn't meaning to be funny. "I have been training for 22 years," he continued, "This program was a great reminder of what not to do. We are in the learning space after all. As eternal learners, our mind is tuned to find learning in every experience. This program helped me reflect on all those things I may also be doing unconsciously, that I should think about and stop."

Here was an entirely new way of processing the same experience! His words have since stayed with me. As I grow older, I see the truth of those words even more. *A facilitator is an eternal learner, who learns from any experience, good or bad.*

As even more years passed, I became more conscious of the difference between training and facilitation. I realized each of them had their place and value in learning, but often were not appropriately used. Most trainers (much like I was some years back) were not even aware that something called 'facilitation' existed. Even if they had heard about it, most had never experienced the power it had. So, it was only fair that they did not explore it further. I wished I could find a way to reach more trainers and let them experience facilitation, so they could use training or facilitation by choice!

I soon got this chance.

It started with a request from a large public sector enterprise. They wanted to conduct a 'Train-the-Trainer' (TTT) for their in-house trainers. The client informed us that this was a very senior group. She also shared that each of the participants would have attended at least 2–3 TTT programs in the last 5 years. "This program would need to be extraordinary to meet their expectations," she cautioned us.

I reached an hour early on the day of the program. I was surprised to see participants were already there. They stood around a table, chatting, and laughing. They seemed to know each other well and had decided to catch up before the program started.

I saw some looks of disbelief as I introduced myself. A few participants were candid enough to say that they were expecting someone more senior. They were used to a formal start, with a

PowerPoint slide announcing the title of a program. I noticed discomfort when they saw none. I decided to use an icebreaker that would allow them to share their feelings and discomfort. This helped build rapport and trust. Right from the ice breaking to the close of the program, I used different facilitative tools and methods that I had learnt over the years. Before they knew it, they were engrossed! The program ended on a high. On the last day, the group was already exploring ways in which they could bring facilitation techniques into their organization.

The reactions of the trainers on that program, helped me recognize the impact of the format and tools I had used. I saw that once trainers experienced facilitation; they took to it like fish to water! "Train-the-Trainer" became one of my favourite programs and I continued to run several of these.

It was the final day of one such Train-the–Trainer program that I was running for a large group of trainers. Participants were working in groups at their tables. I was moving around the room to observe what the groups were doing. They seemed engrossed in their task.

A light-hearted comment from a participant told me I was now using facilitation much more easily. As I neared a table, he turned around to look at me. With a cheeky grin he said, "Nasreen, saara kaam to hum kar rahen hain; aap kya kaam kar rahin hain?!" (Nasreen, we are doing all the work; what work are you doing?!). Finally, I was becoming better at being able to "let go" and trust the group's wisdom. This was one skill that had been hard for me to absorb!

And that facilitators' conference in Chennai that I attended? What did it shift in me?

As I went in and out of the sessions in that conference, I saw the uniqueness and brilliance of each facilitator. I had a Eureka moment in that closing session. I realized that there were many nuances of the craft that I had learnt along the way. I had also made several significant shifts during this journey of being a coach and trainer, but I had not recognized and acknowledged them.

The conference shifted how I saw myself.

It allowed me, finally, to call myself a 'Facilitator'.

The Infinite End

Nasreen Khan

The train had picked up speed. The rhythmic sound of the wheels and the gentle swaying of the carriage allowed my body to relax. Having been an hour into the journey, my mind had now accepted the 6 feet by 2 feet train berth as my home for the night. Settling down to sleep, my thoughts went to the conversation that had brought me here.

A month ago, I had received a call from the Principal of a school in Bhimtal. He explained how difficult it was to maintain the quality of education in that hilly region. "As you know, we are a non-profit school," he started. "Our pay scales are not so good. It becomes tough to get good teachers here. The morale of the teachers is quite low. You will notice that yourself when you meet them. They lack passion and energy. In fact, most of them barely speak up. If we want children here to get educated, we need to inspire these teachers. Could you give them a motivational talk? For 45 minutes to an hour perhaps? Maybe you could also give them some communication tips."

We spoke for over an hour and a half. I wanted to understand the context well. He was very patient, listening deeply, and answering any questions I had. Our conversation ended with my agreeing to visit the school, but not for a one-hour talk. I said I would need two hours at least to conduct a short workshop. He agreed.

When I reached Kathgodam, the school van was waiting to receive me. From there, it would take an hour plus of driving through the winding mountain roads.

At the school, one of the senior teachers escorted me to the venue. Their new auditorium was a large hall with shiny, tiled flooring. There was a stage on one side, and a stack of metal chairs in the other corner. The room had 14 doors, 7 on each side, and an equal number of windows without any panes. There was a playground on the longer side.

"Since there is a power cut every morning, we would need to leave the doors open to let in light" the teacher said. "It may be a bit windy, but we will keep the children away, so there would be less noise. Hope that is all right?" I nodded. I was wondering would I be able hold to the group together in such a large space. And that too when being heard over the wind itself seemed difficult!

The next day, I woke to a breezy and pleasant morning. When I entered the auditorium, most teachers were already there. Some of them were seated, some were standing around chatting. A few looked at me with unconcealed curiosity. While we were waiting, one of the bolder ones asked me why I had made such a "tedious" journey. One even advised, "you should have come next month. That would have been a better time to visit the hills." This was going to be interesting!

We started formally. The principal gave a short welcome speech, introduced me, and set the context for my 'talk'! (he continued to call it a 'talk' despite reminding him several times that it was a workshop). He wished us "good luck" and left.

I started with a simple ice breaker to get them up and moving. They were clearly not used to interacting with each other in this manner. It took much longer for them to loosen up than I expected. But it worked.

It was a full 40 minutes later that I was able to move forward with what I had planned!

Putting them into groups of six, I handed over two blank charts and some marker pens to each group. The instructions for the activity were simple. As a group, they had to answer only one question. They could answer the question as they wished – write, draw, or depict it in any manner. The other rules were that they had to agree as a group on the final response and they had to share how they had arrived at it. They had 40 minutes to do this.

The immediate reactions to this were not at all encouraging.

A senior teacher, who seemed to be the spokesperson for others got up. He said, "Madam, most of us have over 15 years' experience. We are told this from the day we join our first job. Give us something more interesting to do. This, we know." Others were more subtle. They asked if I could share motivational stories instead. A few suggested that I "teach communication skills". They also emphasized they did not need 40 minutes to answer this question, since they 'knew' the answer.

I stood firm, saying we would do other activities, but after this exercise was complete.

They half-heartedly began their discussions.

Most groups started by standing around in a circle, marker pen in hand, ready to complete the answer in a jiffy. As they started talking, discussions became more intense. Some teachers sat down on the floor with the chart papers. Some picked up rough sheets and started scribbling. I noticed calculators on mobile phones being turned on. The energy in the room was shifting. Views were becoming more animated. The principal had to send someone to tell us to lower our voices!

The question put to them was simple:

As a teacher, how many lives do you impact in your lifetime?

After 40 minutes, most teachers were still in deep discussions while two groups were ready with their answer.

The first group gave their number: 3,800,000 lives, they said. They explained their calculations, "Each student influences her family and her friends, and that had a multiplier effect. Since your question said impact, not teach, we included people in the student's circle."

Then, the second group shared their number: 100,700,000 lives. They had included the neighbourhood and society as well. They looked happy with their figure of over one hundred million!

Two teams said it was not possible to calculate a specific number. They explained their reasoning: "We looked at the present environment of a student first. Each student that a teacher teaches today has an impact on his/her family, friends, and society. Then we thought about the future. As a student goes out into the world, his/her sphere of influence widens. As a student starts working, starts a family and becomes a mature citizen, he/she will influence work colleagues (and their families), his/her own family, the society. In fact, he/she will influence the entire expanded ecosystem in some way. He/she will also influence the grandchildren! Then each of those that this student influences will, in turn, influence their stakeholders. And this cycle will continue to repeat.".

"That is why we cannot give you a specific number for lives that we impact in our life as a teacher," they asserted. "It is an infinite number."

An infinite number? That is *infinite lives*, they were talking about.

The senior teacher who had asked for an alternative exercise spoke up again. His voice sounded different. "Since the time I became a teacher 22 years ago, I have been *told* that as teachers we have a huge impact on the students. I always knew that. In fact, I have *told* this to many younger teachers. But today, when we had a chance to discuss this in this manner amongst ourselves, it was different. As new ideas came up, we delved deeper. Even with my experience, I found it difficult to visualize how far and wide our impact reaches. During our discussions, it became more evident that there is no part of life, no part of the world, that we do not touch. I never realized we had so much influence. *We impact the world through the students that we teach!"*

"Trying to calculate a number made it even more obvious," he continued. "We realized we cannot give you a specific number because it was not possible to calculate. Not only is it infinite, but it is also endless. Our influence on one student, passes not only from person to person, but also from generation to generation. It crosses all boundaries. Our calculation is correct. We do impact infinite lives."

As other teachers listened, a hush fell over the room. The enormity of their own contribution was not easy for them to digest.

The principal's words have stayed with me: "If we want children here to get educated, we need to inspire these teachers." That is what had got me on that eight-hour journey that day.

I had also made my own little contribution to infinite lives.

*Teachers affect eternity; no one can tell
where their influence stops.*

– Henry Brook Adams

Power Tips to Help You Fast Forward

"To attain knowledge, add things every day.
To attain wisdom, remove things every day."

– Lao Tzu

Historically, success has been achieved by people who had the desire and the ability to create a positive change. Only if we challenge the status quo will change happen and for it to be positive, we need to listen to others in the field. Since we cannot have so much dialogue, we thought we would put it all in a book for our readers. As we wrote our stories, one thread in all our minds was to get our experiences together in one place for potential facilitators. We wanted to bring in as many diverse anecdotes and 'caselets' for a reader to be able to refer to and apply as and when required. You will see that all the instances are mutually exclusive and collectively exhaustive.

To circumvent the long route of reading and searching through a book for methods, we wanted to create a cheat sheet that would come in handy. A kind of "remedy at a glance" section which could boost up your speed and give you that jumpstart into facilitation.

Understanding What is Group Process Facilitation

Group Process facilitation is the art and science of using the collective wisdom of the group to achieve consensus, by running well-identified and relevant processes. It's about enabling groups to achieve meaningful outcomes.

Look around. At every level of society across the globe and in every organization, groups are seeking ways to address complex issues, resolve conflicts and make good decisions together. Facilitation is a way of working with people. It enables and empowers people to collectively take decisions and move forward.

Facilitation can also be viewed as a developmental and educational method which encourages people to share ideas, resources, opinions, and to think critically in order to identify needs and find effective ways of satisfying those needs.

Facilitators enable a group to bring out the collective wisdom of the group to solve the issue or problem at hand with various processes and methods. They do this by using 'divergence' and 'convergence' of Ideas during the process for gaining holistic consensus. In facilitation, this 'divergence' and 'convergence' are key elements. Divergence is used mainly for 'brain storming' new ideas and possibilities. Convergence is used for filtering out ideas that are not relevant at that point of time to the group and selecting only those ideas which the entire group agrees upon.

Where can Facilitation be used?

Facilitation is a method that can be used in many places & settings, although it is usually used with groups of people to help them achieve consensus. Wherever there is conversation taking place, that needs to be aligned or converged into facilitation can be used.

Examples would include Board Meetings, Training set ups, Strategic planning, Community work, Educational purposes, Political meetings, Sports Coaching, Large community Conventions, Large group Voting, Conflict resolutions, Consensus Building, Problem solving, Goal Setting, Vision building, Change Management, Post Crisis Planning and Handling, and Natural Catastrophe Response strategy building.

Who can use Facilitation?

Everyone!

Users can include Trainers, Teachers, Chairpersons, Team leaders, CEOs of the company, Law Enforcement authorities, Ministry, Sales and Marketing Managers, Facility Managers, Head of Meetings, Community Leaders, and Politicians.

You can use facilitation in every single opportunity where two or more than two people are involved in a directed conversation.

The Value of Facilitation

Some of the core benefits of professional facilitation include the following:

- Efficient use of time and money

Bringing people together, whether face-to-face or for a virtual meeting, has a real cost. Time wasted in unproductive meetings saps morale and prevents participants from fulfilling their other responsibilities. A professional facilitator can help the group accomplish more in less time, eliminating the need for multiple meetings, and generating forward momentum on the issues under discussion.

- Full participation

A good facilitator encourages the participation of all, while managing the tendency for some members of the group to dominate the conversation. They create conditions that support the contribution of those who traditionally say very little and of those whose views diverge from those of the leader or the majority. Full participation, combined with respectful listening, gives the group a more complete understanding of the points of view in the room and a better chance of reaching a sustainable decision.

- Record of results

Dynamic discussions can produce a lot of information and ideas. Without taking sides, the facilitator can summarize various statements in ways that respect all the different voices and help the group identify areas of agreement and issues that are still unresolved.

- Co-creation of outcomes

After eliciting the full spectrum of views and welcoming strong opinions, the facilitator encourages the group to generate previously unconsidered, creative solutions that can resolve apparent differences. The group is then able to craft agreements that all members can support and move forward with a sense of shared ownership.

- Clear buy-in from participants

As the processes driven by the facilitator help the group co-create a meaningful outcome for themselves, the buy-in for the consensus achieved and the decision made is more likely to be upheld and adhered to by the group. In the context of business outcomes, it is their outcomes defined by them which they will achieve at any cost.

Power Tips

These Power Tips will assist your progress towards excellence in facilitation. This is not just theory; these are the learnings from our collective experiences that will serve as a compact reference guide to power up on your journey of facilitation.

Power Tip #1: The Facilitative Mindset

As a facilitator, it will help to adopt a 'servant-leadership' approach. Your purpose is to *help* people reach meaningful conclusions.

Often as a manager or a trainer, you may perceive that you are in control, that you have authority. Authoritative approach as a facilitator does not help the group. What helps the group is for them to realise that they are in control. They need to feel in control of the ideas they exchange, in control of the collective decisions they arrive at. So, let go of control. As you will often hear experienced facilitators say, "let the inmates run the asylum!"

Every-time you facilitate, check if you are ready to let go of the control. You may have the answers. But the answers the group uncovers are the ones that matter. So, focus on the outcomes the group needs help in arriving at; outcome for the group and by the group.

Power Tip #2: Design and Preparation

In our experience, designing and preparation before the session is critical. It has a major contribution to the success of the facilitation effort.

What do you design for? You need to design for the experience you would want the group to go through. Design for the thinking process you want them to go through. Design for bringing out divergence in group thinking. Then design for enabling convergence for the group. You will need to design for ensuring inclusivity.

Flexibility is critical to success as a facilitator. Our experience indicates, design for it. Have a Plan A and Plan B.

Power Tip #3: Ask the Right Questions

As a facilitator, let go of the 'telling mode' and adopt the 'asking mode'. Be careful while framing the questions you ask. Consider what you would want the group to think or do as a result of your asking the question. How will they interpret the question? How will they *feel* about the question?

Once you have prepared your questions, think about *how* you are going to ask the questions. How you ask the questions is just as important as the wording of the question.

Asking questions is a science as well as an art! And this will actually help you progress to the next power tip.

Power Tip #4: Conversational Dialogue

Enabling conversational dialogue within the group is a sign of a well-facilitated session. Conversations allow for a good exchange of thoughts. Conversations bring out divergent ideas into the open. Conversations will also facilitate the convergence of ideas.

Enable conversational dialogue and not a debate. Dialogue is a two-way communication done in a conducive manner. It builds better rapport and relationship.

As a facilitator, get better at inviting people to converse. Enable un-hindered expression of ideas and thoughts. Selection of processes that encourage conversational dialogue helps. Creating a knowledge base of processes helps with this.

Power Tip #5: Build Your Knowledge Base

Try and gain as much knowledge of what 'Group process facilitation' is, as possible. The International Association of Facilitators (IAF-World) is a great community to gain this knowledge. IAF promotes the exchange of knowledge of facilitation. A library of processes that have worked across the globe are available on the IAF web site.

There are other sources that provide a library of processes too. Sessions Lab is one such source. Liberating Structures is another source. Thiagi's books and website are yet another, often used resource.

Power Tip #6: Group Engagement

When facilitating a session, make sure the group is actively engaged. You have to know the pulse of the group. Building a rapport with the group is critical. A facilitator is almost like a 'fly on the wall' and yet, keeps a track of group dynamics.

Social contracting at the start of the facilitative session helps. It creates a consensus on how the group will operate.

Power Tip #7: Holding the Space

Creating a non-threatening environment is a critical element to successful facilitation. In our experience, this is probably the most under-rated, yet critical aspects of facilitation.

As a facilitator, your responsibility is to hold the space for the group to interact freely. No one should hesitate to express their thoughts. Divergence of ideas is best achieved when there is no judgement. And convergence of ideas is achieved through inclusion and mutual respect.

Practical experience shows that exhibiting vulnerability on behalf of the facilitator helps. It shows to the participants that none of us need to be perfect to contribute. All contributions matter.

Power Tip #8: Feedback and Feedforward

As facilitators, each one of us has practiced continuous learning. Irrespective of your experience, be ready to unlearn, learn and re-learn. It is, however, easier said than done.

It helps to have a mentor, or someone who will share feedback and guide you along. IAF holds practice labs – sessions which you can run and get feedback from facilitators with extensive experience. This feedback is based on the competencies laid out by IAF for facilitators. Some of the IAF facilitators run programs on facilitation. As you engage with the IAF community you come to know of such learning opportunities. Genuine Mirror Feedback is the greatest teacher. Surrender to the feedback as it is coming your way. Another way to learn is to observe and share feedback with your peers. Feedback is rewarding for the giver as well as the receiver.

Power Tip #9: Virtual Power

Facilitation on virtual platforms has been practiced for many years now. It has gained prominence due to the new normal coming into play after the Covid-19 pandemic.

Facilitation works very well on virtual platforms. The facilitator in any case is not the hero for the session. Each of the boosters mentioned above work equally well for a virtual platform too.

The key to using a virtual platform effectively is to know:

- The features of the virtual meeting/webinar platform
- 'Social contracting', that enables participants to express themselves
- How to enable brainstorming of ideas using tools like whiteboards, etc.
- How to use multiple virtual medium tools together
- How to facilitate the formation of smaller groups
- How a process debrief can be managed

In our collective experience, the designing and preparation for a virtual session takes more time and effort. The advantage of virtual sessions is that they enable reaching out to people without the constraints of geography.

In Summary

Many a times, we have been asked the question, "What is the key to effective facilitation?" As our experiences show, there is no single key to success as facilitators. Rather, it is more like a combination lock. And these Power Tips will hopefully provide the right combination to unlock your success in your journey ahead.

All the best!

Glossary

- 3D Lab: Design, Develop, Deliver; a format for practicing facilitation and getting feedback on the competencies of a facilitator

- Avoiding Group Think: Avoiding flaws in group decision making

- Concept attainment: Reaching a shared understanding of Issues

- Divergence-convergence: Process of getting diverse ideas and then converging to one or few as agreed upon by the group

- Fish bowl: enables facilitation of large group by focussing on small group discussion, in an inner circle; whilst the rest of the group listens

- Harvesting group wisdom: Using group wisdom to progress the group ahead

- Ice Breakers: Activities for easy group bonding and conversation

- Johari Window: a simple and useful tool for understanding and training self-awareness, personal development, improving communications.

- Kata conversation: Unhurried conversations

- Kirkpatrick Model: A model for analyzing and evaluating the results of training and educational programs

- MECE: Mutually Exclusive Collectively Exhaustive
- Mentimeter – Online tool to capture responses
- NLP: Neuro-Linguistic programming
- ORID: Objective, Reflective, Interpretive, Decisional
- Post its: Small, coloured pieces of paper on which participants write their thoughts and place on the sticky wall for others to read
- Role Playing: Preparing for difficult situations through simulation
- Running effective meetings: Setting an objective and sticking to it
- Social contracting: similar to ways of working
- Sticky wall: A thin plastic sheet with glue on which paper sticks
- Strategy Tools: Tools and Techniques to help you understand your Environment
- TTF: Train the Facilitator
- TTT: Train the Trainer
- Ways of Working: Agreement by the group on how they are going to work together
- Wicked problems: A special category of problems
- WIIFM: What's in it for me? Why should I do it.
- WIFT: What's in it for them? Why should they do it.

The following are processes used during facilitation that have been mentioned in the Stories. Details around them can be found at the

Sessions Lab (www.sessionlab.com/solutions/meeting-facilitation) and the IAF-World website (www.iaf-world.org)

- Affinity Diagrams
- Conversation Caffe
- Dot Voting
- Exercise Sparks
- Fish Bone Analysis
- Force Field Analysis
- Gallery Walk
- I do Art
- Lotus Blossom
- The Value Spectrum

Acknowledgements

We would like to acknowledge the community of Facilitators, our Mentors and everyone who supported us in the journey of putting this book together.

Introduction

www.ingramcontent.com/pod-product-compliance
Lightning Source LLC
Chambersburg PA
CBHW020905180526
45163CB00007B/2633